HOW TO PRAY THE SHAMAN'S WAY

HOW TO PRAY THE SHAMAN'S WAY

ANCIENT TECHNIQUES
FOR EXTRAORDINARY RESULTS

JOSÉ LUIS STEVENS, PhD

Hierophantpublishing

Cover design by Emma Smith

Cover art by Dusan Petkovic || Shutterstock and
Subin Pumsom || Shutterstock

Illustration by Alila Medical Media || Shutterstock

Part Page Illustration by Elena Shchukina || Shutterstock

Print book interior design by Frame25 Productions

Hierophant Publishing
8301 Broadway, Suite 219
San Antonio, TX 78209
www.hierophantpublishing.com

If you are unable to order this book from your local
bookseller, you may order directly from the publisher.

Library of Congress Control Number: 2021930755
ISBN: 978-1-950253-12-8

10 9 8 7 6 5 4 3 2 1

Dedication

This book is dedicated to all my teachers
who taught me something about prayer.

Guadalupe Candelario
Rafael Candelario
Maria Candelaria Lopez
Herlinda Augustine Fernandez
Enrique Sinuiri Flores
Mahatma Gandhi
Paramahansa Yogananda
Jesus of Nazareth
Thomas Merton
Teresa of Avila
Siddhartha Gautama (The Buddha)
Satnam Khalsa
Babaji
Patanjali
Rumi
Thich Nhat Hanh
Sri Aurobindo
Dalai Lama
Tulku Urgyen Rinpoche
Zen Master Seung Sanime

Lewis Bostwick
Paul Selig
Sergio Magana
Lao Tzu
Black Elk
Pachamama
All my allies
And innumerable others

Prayer for Peace

Thank you, Spirit, for
manifesting peace in our world.
Thank you for teaching me how to be peaceful.
Thank you for the peace I feel inside now.
May I be a catalyst for peace in the world.
May I live peacefully.
I Am at peace, *I Am* at peace.

Contents

Foreword

Under a blanket of stars, a shaman gazes into a deep, still pool of water. In the moonlight, the reflection of the shaman's face and the night sky shines back. The shaman asks aloud, "What is inside this reflection, this mirror of me?"

He hears a response that comes from both inside and outside of himself: "You are the same as all the stars above you. You are present in the whole universe. The energy that is inside them is inside of you—as you and the universe are one."

In prayer, the shaman makes a conscious effort to align herself with the energy of Life, because at the deepest level, she knows that all is one. The art of prayer is in the expression of this ancient truth through word, gesture, and movement. This rich practice, performed by countless voices over millennia in every culture on Earth, finds renewed vitality in José Stevens's beautiful book.

The Toltec tradition to which I belong shares many of the perspectives this book discusses on the varied purposes of prayer:

As medicine. Prayer exists in every language, every tribe, every tradition. When it comes from the heart, prayer can send potent healing energy to or from the one who prays.

In service. Just as trees are in service to life—giving fruit, shade, energy, and support—the act of prayer is a service to all beings, nurturing positive energy, compassion, relationship, and kindness.

As gratitude. In prayer, we honor the power of Being and give thanks for the miracle of our existence. Prayer focuses us and reminds us to appreciate and celebrate our most valuable gift—the vibrancy of life that radiates through and around us in every given moment.

As remembrance. The shaman knows that the ancestors and elders who have moved beyond this world live on within us, walking alongside us throughout our whole life. Prayer offers the opportunity to reach across time and space to honor their wisdom and guidance, knowing that one day we will become ancestors ourselves.

As wisdom. Through prayer, we ask for clarity in finding the answers that are most often already inside us. We drink in the nectar of the flower that is our memory, experience, and intuition. Prayer creates the space for us to remember who we truly are.

As both a question and its answer. In a time of need, in a time of pain, in a time of doubt, prayer gives us the strength to overcome life's challenges. In prayer we often ask questions, but the shaman knows that the act of praying is, in itself, an answer.

And finally:

Prayer is a seed. A seed is potential energy. All energy needs a container, and prayer is that container. The shaman goes inside herself, creates and focuses her intent, and then releases it into the living world through word, movement, ritual, or song. When we shift the power of our intent toward the manifestation of good things for the world and then surrender ourselves to the flow of life without attachment to outcomes, it is not so rare to find that the Universe steps in to help in surprising and unexpected ways.

In my tradition, I am a *Nagual* (shaman) in the Eagle Knight lineage, but in my view, a shaman can be *anyone who prays from the heart and for the benefit of all beings*. As a shaman, you understand that your whole life is the prayer. You are acquainted with the energy of life itself. Your finely tuned intent controls and creates a beautiful dream, so that whatever stories you tell hold the fruit of your awareness, the vision of what is inside the reflection in the water. Your stories remind others that they too are expressions of this dynamic and magnificent energy of life.

We are each of us no different than Jesus, Moses, Buddha, or all the great masters of India—another thing I love about this book is that José draws from the wisdom of many different traditions. We have all been given the ability to sharpen our awareness and hone our intent—to use our gifts to craft our lives into living works of art and to help others do the same. We are all children of the same Mother Earth, and prayer is the Mother's way. It is in this nurturing of love through prayer that we heal, honor, and serve the Mother every single time we gather our thoughts, lift our hands, light our candles, or raise our voices in celebration, thanksgiving, supplication, or petition.

I can think of no better place to begin the deeply transformative journey into the power of shamanic prayer than this book.

—don José Ruiz

Introduction

Sky our Grandfather,
Moon our Grandmother,
Earth our Mother.
I Am thankful
We love each other.
We are grateful.
—Cherokee prayer

He was a weathered dark-skinned older man and we watched him with curiosity as he trudged up the trail toward us leading his gray sugarcane-laden donkey. Although his clothing was little more than faded rags blistered by the bright sun, we noticed purpose in his stride and intensity in his expression. Eventually, he reached us—two *Norte Americanos* sitting on a grassy slope in the middle of the remote Huichol territory in the Sierra mountains of Mexico. Without hesitation, he squatted down, looked into our eyes, and, without blinking, asked in excellent Spanish: "And what has God told you today?"

I was completely taken by surprise. Where else does a stranger greet you like this? I mumbled some response (I don't remember what) as he got right to the point: "I'll tell you what God told me today!"

With that, he began a most surprising and informative discourse about the state of the planet, what was to come in the future, and what we needed to do about it. He spoke of very difficult world events, extreme challenges for mankind, environmental destruction, climatic and weather changes, war, and economic distress. "We must all learn to pray," he declared, "and if we do, we will receive the help we need to see these times through!"

This man was in no way a raving lunatic. He maintained eye contact and spoke with eloquence and authority. I realized we were in the presence of a Huichol holy man, and I knew from my studies with shamans that this was not a chance encounter.

My wife, Lena, and I had been on our way to a Huichol fertility ceremony in a nearby village when we met this man. Our host, who had managed to obtain permission for us to participate in the usually forbidden ceremony, approached and interrupted our meaningful exchange with the old man, motioning to us that it was time to go. When we asked him about the old Huichol, he laughed and told us that, indeed, he was one of their respected holy men who was known for his predictions and prophecies.

This serendipitous encounter was to have a deep impact on me and has stayed with me for many years. I have not forgotten the old man's admonition to pray regularly and, as a result of doing so, I have written this book. Despite our brief encounter, this holy man had an influential hand in its contents.

Foundations

One of my earliest memories is sitting through Mass between my parents unable to see over the pew in front of me. I could hear the drone of Latin, the occasional bells, and the coughs, sneezes, and shuffling of the congregation. Blocked from participating in a more meaningful way, I found myself contemplating my own existence and became totally intrigued by the fact that I was alive and conscious of myself. I knew I had not created myself, nor did I remember being created. Yet as I contemplated the miracle of being alive here in the present moment, I found myself delighted in the flow of consecutive moments that buoyed me along like a boat on a river of awareness. I became transfixed by an awareness of a single truth: "I am alive! I am alive! I am alive!" I felt like the luckiest person on Earth.

I don't remember how long this ecstasy lasted, nor do I remember now if I experienced it many times or only once. What I do know is that I have spent a great deal of my life attempting to get back to that state of original awe and those early pristine moments of pure prayer. Now, in my early seventies, I am finally recapturing that awareness of being alive. Nothing more. So simple, so true, so liberating.

Until I reached the age of seven, I was fortunate to live in a house in East Hollywood surrounded by a mix of palms, eucalyptus, and other assorted tall trees. The place seemed like a forest filled with birds right in the middle of a busy city. My great love at the time was to climb one particular tree in front of our house—a tree with many branches, smooth bark, and the shiniest green leaves I had ever seen. I often climbed this tree and perched in a favorite cleft between two branches, remaining there for hours and communing with the tree. Just as in church, I felt an extraordinary sense of aliveness there, contemplating my own awareness and my consciousness of the tree and the many birds that came to perch and sing there. There, I communed daily with my Creator in a state of perfect happiness.

As a child, the outdoors was my favorite place to play and to contemplate, and that I did with great abandon. In these carefree days, no one ever taught me to talk to God or Spirit. It just happened naturally, as if I had always known what to do. I also spent a great deal of time as a child just listening. I believe that Spirit talked to me then, but I now have no recall of what I was told.

In these earliest years of my childhood, I spent a lot of time with my Mexican grandmother, Maria, whom I called Nana. At her knee, I learned many strange and wonderful things about the indigenous peoples of Mexico who, as servants in her family's hacienda, had raised her and taught her their lore and traditional ways. Through the powerful stories she told me in Spanish, Nana introduced me to the world of shamans and the miraculous healings performed by the Toltecs of Old Mexico.

Although one of my parents was Protestant and the other Catholic, I was raised in the Catholic Church and spent many hours participating in its rituals—singing in the choir, studying my catechism and Bible history, and learning prayers. During my school years, those prayers consisted of rote memorization and obligations given to me in confession as punishment for my sins. As a practicing Catholic, the fear of sin and hellfire was drummed into me, and as I grew older, I gradually lost the magic awareness of being alive and created by God that had brightened my early years. For decades, I didn't seem to be able to recapture the profound awareness and joy that I had enjoyed for the first few years of my life. By the time I reached my late teens, I found myself so alienated from Catholicism that I no longer attended church and gave up prayer altogether.

Clearly my experience of religion as a path to aliveness had not taken me where I needed to go. I became progressively less aware, more fearful, and more despairing. As I look back now, however, I see that, despite setbacks, that experience gave me a foundation of mysticism on which I would later build a deep and personal connection with Spirit.

The Road Home

For the last forty years, I have studied with a number of powerful shamans from various parts of the world, particularly from Mexico and Peru. My wife and I were apprenticed for over ten years to Guadalupe Candelario, a wonderful Huichol *maracame* (shaman) from the Sierras of central Mexico. Although he was illiterate, Guadalupe had a better grasp of Spirit than anyone I have ever met, before or since. He had true respect for the Creator and lived his life in absolute harmony with his values and his understanding of how Spirit works in nature and within people. He taught us that *El Dios*, as he called God, would answer all questions and provide a clear path. In order for this to happen in the most effective way, however, we must talk to God regularly in a deeply private way and with an absolutely open heart. This, I eventually found, was the key to powerful and "accelerated prayer," or prayer that produces results quickly. Accelerated prayer may not enable me to make changes in the world—although it quite often does—but it always brings about positive changes in me.

When Guadalupe spoke of God, tears ran freely down his cheeks. He was truly a holy man who opened up new worlds of awareness in me. He explained that, when I was a child, I had been open to God and nothing stood between us. Over time, however, I became burdened with beliefs that closed me off from God. As a child, before life came hurtling in to challenge me, I had been shown what was possible and that awareness remained strong within me, calling me back to Spirit. And this is exactly the way it happened. The light that brightened my early years has become a beacon that illuminates my personal journey. And that light is stronger now than ever.

When I was twenty-eight and traveling in India, I met a powerful guru who told me that I would one day become a writer and author many books that would be of great benefit to the people who read them. At the time, I dismissed his prediction as highly improbable. But with time, I have come to appreciate what he had to say. I now *do* write books in the hope that Spirit will work through them to bring the most benefit to the greatest number of people. It is my greatest wish to be a vehicle for Spirit and to help bring people back to their original relationship with God. I wish to renew their ability to pray to Spirit, to affirm what is positive, and to discover their own power—each in his or her own way. May this book fulfill that intent.

Shamanism

The primary source for this book is shamanism, the world's most ancient nature-based and cross-cultural spiritual path. Shamanism teaches that Spirit is everywhere and in everything. This belief, which has become my primary spiritual path, is highly compatible with many religions because most of them—including Hinduism, Tibetan Buddhism, Taoism, and even Catholicism—have incorporated many shamanic traditions and practices into their faith. For example, the Catholic Mass and baptism are highly shamanic in every respect.

The term *shaman* originated with the Evenki tribe in Siberia and means "he or she who sees in the dark or sees what is hidden." It has evolved to describe indigenous people with extraordinary abilities who practice the tenets of shamanism throughout the world. Shamans are typically trained through a long and difficult apprenticeship as leaders, healers, ceremonialists, artists, storytellers, and wisdom seekers. Moreover, shamanic insight and understanding about the nature of reality have been verified by many of the findings of quantum physics. There are even those who say—and I agree—that the future belongs to the marriage of shamanic practice and scientific discovery.

Much of what I have learned about prayer has come from various shamanic teachers with whom I have spent many years, listening and integrating their wisdom. Other teachers have come to me through books—those whose lives were ended before I was born, but who had profound knowledge to impart. But perhaps my most important instruction has come from my own inner dialogues with Spirit, from moments of deep contemplation, and from states of heightened awareness, especially in nature.

Most of the prayers presented in this book were downloaded from Essence or Source, given to me in moments of deep contemplation in nature. A few are age-old prayers that I have modified for my own use or updated to make them more accessible. Because everyone is connected to Spirit, these prayers belong to everyone. They have been given in one form or another to millions of people throughout history.

Think of them as free software that anyone can use, and feel free to alter them, add to them, and reformulate them to suit your own needs. They are intended only as guidelines and suggestions to help you get started creating your own powerful prayers.

In all of these prayers, you can call on God using any name you like—Great Spirit, Great Mother or Father, God the Father, Allah, Spirit, Brahma, Vishnu, Shiva, Buddha, Krishna, Rama, Creator, Provider, Source, All that Is, and many others. I have used the words God, Creator, Spirit, Essence, and Provider interchangeably throughout the text. Although different religions may have distinct theological definitions for each of these terms, here they refer to the same thing: the Creator and Source of the Universe.

How to Use This Book

This book has three aims. The first is to describe the seven perspectives or "ways" of prayer. Only when you fully understand these can you choose the one best suited to your needs in the moment. The second is to suggest ways of praying that promote well-being and build power following the shaman's path. The third is to give you a number of effective prayers that you can build on to create your own personal prayers. My goal is to empower you to become a person who prays regularly for the greater benefit of yourself and the world at large. By praying well, we can help the world evolve more quickly from primitive conflict to the life-supporting and empowering activities that are our birthright.

This is both a book *about* prayer and a book *of* prayer. Its purpose is to show you how prayer works from a shamanic perspective and to share ways in which you can use prayer to lift your life into a higher expression of well-being on every level.

To that end, we will explore the different spiritual perspectives out of which prayer may arise and discuss ways to prepare yourself for prayer emotionally, spiritually, and physically. I recommend that you read this book all the way through and then go back to the chapters that call to you and you feel will be most beneficial to you. For example, once you feel that you have a firm understanding of the basics of prayer and its perspectives, you may choose to go directly to the chapter on healing (chapter 8) or the one on dealing with fears (chapter 7). If one area of your life is more in need of prayer than another, feel free to skip to the chapter that is most relevant to your personal situation. If you are like me and most people I know who follow this path, your life circumstances will change and you may find that you need to focus on a different chapter in the future. By reading the book cover to cover first, you can plant seeds that will call to you when the time is right.

Throughout this book, I emphasize the power of the phrase *I Am* (see in particular chapters 3 and 11). These words of power embody the connection to Spirit in which the entire shamanic tradition is grounded and on which the power of shamanic prayer is based. This phrase expresses the relationship we all enjoy with the Creator and the part we play in the cocreation of our lives. To underscore the importance of these words and to remind you of their power, I have italicized them and capitalized them throughout this book and in the prayers I give you at the end of each chapter. By using this phrase often and with reverence as you pray, you will validate your oneness with Spirit and increase the effectiveness of your prayers.

As you move through this book, please remember that all the prayers and practices included in it are intended to provide inspiration and guidance. But prayers that come from your deepest heart and in your own words can be just as powerful, if not more so, than any prayer you may read in a book. The prayers in this book may move you and you may want to pray with them exactly as they are written. But you may also feel moved to make changes in them to suit your personal circumstances, tradition, or worldview.

And this is absolutely fine. Your personal prayers will create a powerful connection between you and the vibrant, ever-loving, and ever-present Spirit of the Universe.

PART ONE

EMPOWERING YOUR PRAYERS

Chapter 1

What Is Prayer?

Prayers outlive the lives of those who uttered them;
outlive a generation; outlive an age; outlive a world.

—E. M. Bounds

P rayer is an intensely personal communication with what may be considered a higher source of power. For some, this power source is a vague notion of something greater than themselves; for others, it is a specific idea or experience of a God or Creator; for many, it is a clearly defined deity or saint. Despite what some people think, however, it is not necessary to believe in any specific deity for prayer to produce results.

Prayers speak to all the most intense human experiences, including entreaties for material benefits, supplications for blessings, and requests for opportunities. Prayers can be used to honor Spirit, unburden grief, release guilt, unload affliction, support worship, affirm desires, offer gratitude, reduce pain and suffering, and ensure a certain future. While most organized religions include specific prayers in their form of worship, religion is by no means the sole purview of prayer. People the world over rely on prayer, regardless of whether or not they are religious. We know from anthropological studies that prayer is one of humankind's oldest activities, one that is as prevalent today as it has been throughout human history. People of all races, genders, creeds, and cultures pray in many forms and styles.

Despite all that is written about prayer, many people still do not realize that it is a science as well as an art. In fact, there are ways to pray that are more effective than others. And there are some styles of prayer that are downright destructive, as you will see.

Shamans and indigenous peoples believe that prayer is more than the speaking of words; it is a way of living life. Indeed, they believe that life itself is a prayer. Gathering and preparing herbs, cooking, building shelters, or visiting relatives should all be done in the spirit of prayer. Indeed, there is a kind of universal agreement that prayer is something that can be lived as well as spoken. It is a way of being, a perspective, a profoundly personal and sacred orientation to the world. Virtually all the world's great spiritual teachers and mystics have stated, in one fashion or another, that unceasing prayer brings the greatest results.

While we usually think of prayer as a one-way monologue with the Creator, or with Spirit, powerful prayers always end with listening. As I learned from my mentor Don Guadalupe, the listening part of prayer creates a dialogue or two-way stream of communication. And this is one of the definitions of effective prayer. After listening to and dialoguing with Spirit, we must then put whatever we learned into action. That is Spirit in action.

Tips for Praying Successfully

Here are some simple tips on how to pray for maximum benefit. After all, if we are going to spend some of our lives praying, why not make the most of that time by praying effectively?

Stay Present

State your prayers in the present tense, as if the object of your focus were already true. This gives them greater power. You cannot pray from yesterday, nor can you pray from tomorrow, because neither exist in the present moment. Shamanically speaking, you can alter the nature of past events and heal them, but you can only do this from the present. Likewise, you can include your future self in your prayers, but you can only do this from the here and now. From the shamanic perspective, *now* is the moment of power, even though we each have a story or narrative that includes the past and the future. But for all practical purposes, the past and the future are fictional from a shamanic point of view. We have only the present moment to work with.

Tibetan Buddhists, who practice a form of shamanism called *Bon*, say that there are three demons that struggle within each of us. The first is regrets from the past, with all their accompanying guilt, sadness, and anger. The second is the notion of a future that we hope to control. The third is a tendency to be distracted, to let our attention wander, and to focus on something other than the present moment. In other words, it is possible to be in the present moment but still lack the ability to harness the power of prayer. To tap the fullest potential of prayer and the power of the here and now, we must learn to grapple successfully with these three demons and pray from a place of focused attention on the present moment. In other words, the present moment is all we've got. The good news is that it lasts forever. And that means that we have all the time we need to take care of business.

Pray from the Heart

Emotional intensity provides the fuel that propels prayers and affirmations into reality. The ability to feel the emotions associated with our prayers is essential to praying successfully. As you utter your prayer's words, you must simultaneously feel them in your heart and body. For example, I have never seen a Huichol pray without shedding tears, because when Huichols pray they engage their hearts fully.

Intellectual or logical thinking is not really an aspect of prayer. From a shamanic standpoint, thinking is good for doing your taxes or trying to figure out what is wrong with your car, but it is not a very powerful platform from which to work when it comes to prayer. Obviously, thinking has its place in our lives. But trying to think logically about everything is a lot like trying to use a hammer when a screwdriver or a wrench or a saw would do the job much better.

Repetitive rote prayers can be less effective because they were written by others for another time and place. Thus they may not move you in the same way that a spontaneous prayer from your heart does—one that addresses your needs in the moment. In my own case, I remember when I used to say the Lord's Prayer over and over as fast as I could, because it was given as a penance in the confessional. Talk about a lack of power!

Pray with Clarity

Prayers that are clear, unequivocal, concise, and focused produce the best results. While spontaneous prayer can be powerful, prayers should not consist of a confused babble. Your prayers should be focused and clear and state an intention that makes sense. They should not contain a lot of excess words that tend to distract the mind.

If you are confused about the intention of your prayers, you won't be able to muster the power they need to produce results. Consider a prayer that says something like: "Well, I don't know if you are there or not God. Maybe you can help me, maybe not. I don't really know what I need. I just feel miserable about my life. I don't even know if you are there listening or not." This is really more like confused complaining or rambling on in a directionless fashion than it is like praying. Compare that to a prayer like this, which is far clearer and more direct, and has more power: "I am miserable and I am sick of it. I don't know how to get out of this mess, but I know I need help right now. And even though I'm angry, I'm listening."

Pray with Certainty

Make sure your prayers leave no room for doubt. When you pray without giving any attention or energy to doubt, you affirm your trust in Spirit, thereby sending affirmative energy to manifest what your soul desires.

Certainty is not always easy to achieve, however. When you feel uncertain, try borrowing certainty from something you are sure about. "I am certain that the sky is cloudy right now." "I am certain that I have my shoes on." "I am certain that my name is Susan and that I live in Baltimore." At least you know whether these things are true or not. Take a few moments to examine what it feels like when you are absolutely sure that something is true. Then begin a prayer that mimics that feeling, even though you may be uncertain to whom you are speaking. "I know I am saying these words." "I am thankful that I have a dog." "I am thankful that there is a sun in the sky and I feel warm." "I know I have not been feeling well lately and I know I want to feel well again." "I know I am feeling a little better just saying this prayer and I find that interesting." Focus on the things you know are true right now. Then gradually allow that sense of certainty to bleed over into other aspects of your prayer. Doubt lets energy leak out of your prayers. Certainty stops that leak and is an important element of effective prayer.

Pray with I Am

The phrase *I Am* is not only a statement of presence; it is also a recognition of the Spirit within. When you say *I Am*, you acknowledge that whatever you are stating is already true. Each one of us is a multi-dimensional being who exists outside of time and space, as well as within the fiction of time and space. Outside of time, we have no story, but exist in our fullness as creations of Spirit. Outside of space, we have no physical body, but exist as beings in higher dimensional states.

Self-realization and enlightenment thus only make sense in a space-time continuum. When we work toward these states of being, it implies that we are not already in these states, and that only makes sense in the narrow confines of being human. The truth is that we are *already* self-realized and enlightened beings, even though we pretend we are not. *I Am* acknowledges what is so. What if we gave up our struggle to achieve enlightenment or joy? What if all we had to do was realize that we were already there? Now that would be powerful. That would be effortless. That would be amazing.

Pray with Inspiration

Prayers that are inspirational, dramatic, and luminous are most powerful. No one denies that the speeches of Martin Luther King Jr. were incredibly moving, inspiring, and effective. They moved throngs of people to march for and demand social change and equality. King had a gift for cadence and repetition that is often demonstrated by Southern Baptist preachers. Even if you don't agree with the content of their sermons, it is hard to deny how powerful and rousing they can be.

Likewise our own prayers should move us. They should carry us. They should reflect our sincerity and vulnerability. If we imbue our prayers with a little passion and inspiration, we can give them more life than recited prayers that are said half asleep. I have often heard very ordinary people stand up and talk to Spirit with such feeling that I have been moved to tears. There is nothing quite like listening to someone's heartfelt prayer to make you hope it will be answered in fullness by Spirit.

Pray with Intent and Vision

When prayers are accompanied by firm intent and clear vision, they attract the most powerful results. Strong intent enables the dynamic prayer of power. When you see the object of your prayer actively coming about, you know you are praying with great power. In fact, your prayers don't need to have any words at all if your vision is clear and accompanied by strong emotion. Forget the trappings. See yourself giving birth to a child, or marching up to receive your diploma, or saving lives as a physician, or giving powerful speeches that change the world—all without saying anything. And if you do want to say something, let it be: "Make it so!" That is a potent and effective—and quintessentially simple—prayer.

Listen

Sometimes we are so interested in hearing ourselves talk that we fail to do the most important thing of all—listen. Prayers that end with quiet meditation, contemplation, or listening are highly effective, because they can result in a two-way conversation.

Spirit is not generally long-winded. When I have heard Spirit speak within me, it has usually been brief and succinct—perhaps just a phrase or a couple of words. I have heard: "So, go ahead." I have heard: "You are so loved and blessed." I have heard: "What is stopping you?" And when I voiced my doubts, I have heard: "So what?"

Spirit gets right to the point—no muss, no fuss. It usually speaks in a voice that has a searing truthful quality to it; but at the same time, it is kind and supportive, never punitive. Spirit never puts you down. It never belittles. It is never angry or mean. It never attacks. If you experience any of these things, you are most likely not hearing the voice of Spirit, but rather the voice of your own ego. After your prayer, always leave a little silence. You may just be rewarded with a little vision of a thumbs-up.

Act

Whenever possible, take some kind of action to support your prayer. Prayers that are followed by some kind of action or application have the greatest possibility of bringing quick results. Sometimes what we yearn for may require many steps to accomplish. Learning a language takes time. Learning to play a musical instrument takes practice. Getting a black belt takes commitment. Break down the steps necessary to manifest your intent into baby steps, and then just take the first one.

This is a bit like priming a pump. Watch a movie in the language you want to learn. Listen to some flute music if that is the instrument you want to play. Research dojos online and find one in your area. Just take the smallest first step to support your prayer. If what you desire is what is best for you, the next steps will fall into place naturally and without struggle. You will be led from one action to the next, until you have met your objective.

Chapter 2

Seven Perspectives on Prayer

We do not go into ceremony to talk about God.
We go into ceremony to talk to God.
—Chief Quanah Parker

For twenty-six years, Shipibo elders Enrique Arevalo and Herlinda Flores have been my wife's and my primary shamanic teachers. The Shipibo, a tribe from the upper reaches of the Amazon in Peru, are considered authorities in shamanic singing and ceremonial healing. Members of other tribes go to study with them, and my wife and I have made more than forty trips to their village for this purpose. Herlinda, who passed on a number of years ago, was a powerful and outspoken woman known throughout her tribe for her vast knowledge of *icaros*, sacred songs, which she sang with great gusto and flair. She and her husband Enrique spoke of prayer often and helped to shape my understanding of the shamanic perspective on prayer.

Throughout history, missionaries from many different religions have come to the Amazon to impose their faith on the native tribes. Some, unfortunately, have tried to prohibit their Shipibo converts from singing the sacred songs that drive their shamanic rituals. I remember one morning, about 5:00 a.m., when, just as we were finishing an all-night ceremony that had been graced by many powerful *icaros*, we began to hear stylized hymns accompanied by an organ coming faintly from a missionary church nearby. We listened for a bit and then Herlinda said—to no one in particular and in a kind of sad and appalled way— "Those songs have no power, no energy." It was evident to me from what I heard that she was absolutely right. The voices sounded dreary and thin, with no punch whatsoever. After the powerful night of ceremony and the robust shamanic singing that I had just experienced, the songs emanating from the church sounded like elevator music. Beside the Shipibo *icaros*, they sounded dead.

This taught me something very important. You cannot strip away a tribe's culture and replace it with a substitute, and then expect that tribe to thrive. In this case, the singing that supported the foreign faith was very different from the sacred singing the Shipibo had learned from nature, from the plants and animals with whom they shared the environment, and, most important, from the Spirit who had taught them how to care for themselves.

Herlinda's brother, Juan, had been governor of the Shipibo tribe for a number of years and, as we got to know him, he welcomed us and thanked us for helping to bring others to study the Shipibo ways and to join in their ceremonies. Although Juan was short of stature, he radiated power and charisma and, when he could, he joined us in rituals that use the ayahuasca vine for healing. Wearing his long *kushma*, a ceremonial robe, he often stood throughout the entire ceremony and, at intervals, expounded on the Shipibo perspective and their spiritual outlook. One evening, he gave a spontaneous talk on prayer that has stayed with me over the years. In it, he described the various reasons why many who pray for all kinds of things are not successful in those prayers.

For example, Juan spoke of those who pray for a good love life or for bad things to happen to their enemies. But these prayers, he claimed, only create more problems for them because their minds are not in the right place. You must have a pure heart and a firm intention in order for your prayers to succeed, he warned, because prayers don't just automatically produce results unless you participate in helping those results manifest. When you pray in the right way from the right place, however, almost anything becomes possible if you are patient. Although I don't remember all the things Juan said, I do know that his observations have stayed with me and have reinforced lessons that I learned from Guadalupe, our Huichol mentor.

Gradually, both the Huichol and Shipibo teachings about prayer became clearer to me, and I was able to apply them, along with other teachings, to develop an overall philosophy and understanding of prayer. And this is what I offer you in this book.

Perspectives That Drive Prayer

The attitude you bring to your prayers is immensely important in determining their outcome. The values and perspectives that support your prayers reflect your beliefs about your life and the nature of God. Do you believe that God punishes and judges or that God is loving and forgiving? Do you believe that people are miserable sinners or that they are extremely fortunate creations of Spirit? Do you believe that Spirit is distant and separate from humanity or that it is ever-present within? These are exceptionally important questions, because they all influence the outcome you expect from your prayers and how they will make you feel.

While no one can judge another's values, it is clear that different values drive prayers differently. Moreover, different prayers reflect different worldviews and different levels of expansiveness and sophistication. I believe that there is a direct relationship between the worldview of some types of prayer—the notions they contain of others, their diversity, their variety—and their level of expansiveness and effectiveness. And this relationship reflects the evolution of nature itself. From a naturalist perspective, an entire mountain is more complex than a grain of sand, since it comprises different communities of plants and animals, different weather patterns, and different ecosystems.

Below, I give you examples of seven perspectives from which people often pray. After each one, I suggest questions that may help you reflect on your own beliefs and approaches to prayer and some actions you can take to improve your life and the effectiveness of your prayers. If you enjoy keeping a journal, you may wish to write down your answers to these questions. If not, simply be willing to give each question some thought as you move through each perspective.

Before you begin, however, it may be useful to ponder this more general question: Why aren't people more tolerant of the philosophies that others use when they pray? Think about how uncomfortable you feel when someone leads you in a prayer that contradicts your own values. I certainly find it difficult to follow someone who prays for deliverance from damnation and eternal hellfire or who prays to overcome or destroy enemies. These prayers violate my beliefs.

Once you've considered this, ask yourself why prayer is so controversial. Even though most people pray regularly in some fashion, many of these prayers are profoundly different one from the other. In fact, prayers have been so fundamentally different at various times in history that people have killed one another over their form, style, and content. People have even been burned at the stake because their prayers were not acceptable to the authorities of the time.

From a shamanic point of view, the primary cause of friction over prayer is *perception*—the way people see their world—although there are many other contributing factors, including political, racial, and cultural pressures. The seven perspectives, or states of perception, given below, along with their accompanying value systems, lead to different forms of prayer that are often antagonistic to each other because they are driven by the vastly different beliefs about reality to which people in every culture around the world subscribe.

I want to make it clear, however, that while I am not saying it is wrong for people to pray in their own ways, I am saying that there are different levels of sophistication, different levels of effectiveness, and different outcomes for each. While this book focuses more on perspectives that cultivate personal spiritual power—oneness, healing, and compassion—this doesn't mean that everyone should be or is currently interested in that outcome. All prayer perspectives reflect human emotion, human need, and at their core, a desire to connect with God. Moreover, you may find yourself identifying with several of these perspectives simply because we are incredibly complex creatures capable of holding different worldviews and adhering to different values at the same time—sometimes even seemingly contradictory ones. Each of us is made up of a complex of characteristics that clamor for attention and gratification. It is up to you to determine which one suits you and your current situation best.

Some of the perspectives below may seem negative to you. For instance, prayers that petition for the defeat of our enemies are counterproductive if our intent is ultimately to create a kinder and more compassionate world. But remember that all prayer arises out of the depth and range of human experience. By becoming aware of these different experiences and reflecting on our own relationship to them, we grow better equipped to pray more effectively and powerfully. As you move through these perspectives, consider the different kinds of prayer to which you have felt drawn in your life. If you find that you have trouble relating personally to a perspective, consider what experiences may have led others to pray from it, such as their religious affiliation, cultural norms, socioeconomic status, social conditions they may have been in such as war, or a host of other factors.

Kill my enemies. Make me strong over them.

This is a difficult prayer perspective for many of us to understand. Ultimately, it reflects a basic survival instinct to which we may relate at various times in our lives. "I want to survive at all costs and I need help from the gods to be strong and smite my enemies."When I was a child in grade school, there were several bullies who regularly made my life miserable. They taunted me, stole my books, took my bicycle, and generally harrassed me. I prayed to the saints and God to protect me from them and, I must admit, to make them pay for what they were doing. But by praying for harm to my enemies, I merely affirmed my own helplessness and perhaps ran the risk of creating more negative karma for myself.

Prayers of conflict can be found in a variety of traditions—for example, in several famously difficult biblical psalms. Prayers of this sort are often self- or community-centered. Shamanically speaking, however, they have little power to effect change or to make a difference.

This survival perspective derives from a spiritual worldview wherein God/the gods are squarely "on the side" of those praying and will therefore help them triumph over anything that threatens them. Prayers from this perspective are most often based in terror and separation. I don't personally recommend this prayer perspective, and it is not a part of my own shamanic tradition. But it is important to consider the historical perspective of communities that may have faced situations that elicited this kind of terror and this kind of fear for survival. We have all been there at one time or another.

Reflection and Action

- Have you ever prayed from this perspective? Have you ever prayed from a place of fear for your life or for those you love? If not, can you imagine a situation in which you might feel tempted to do so?

- Because fear has a tendency to beget even more fear, find ways you can commit to lessening fear and conflict in your own life, in the lives of those around you, and in the greater world.

Please don't punish me! Save me!

This prayer perspective is akin to the perspective of a child to its parent. Sometimes it translates into something like this: "Please don't punish me for being bad and breaking the rules. Take care of me. Save me from evil and satanic forces or demons that I cannot fight off without your protection." As a child in a Catholic school, I was often told that I was sinful and would go to hell unless I went to confession and said prayers of restitution. I begged God to forgive me and asked for mercy over and over, thinking that I might be spared the everlasting fires of damnation if I did so.

This perpective reflects a kind of personal helplessness that, like the perspective given above, comes from fear. Shamanically speaking, this kind of prayer takes the power away from the person praying and places it all in the hands of a parental God—a God who is sometimes powerful and angry and may mete out punishment.

On occasion, however, we may need the intervention of a *loving* parent to help us in our hour of need. Sometimes we need to be soothed, consoled, or assured that we are okay. Asking Spirit to hold us in our vulnerability or in times of intense suffering can be extraordinarily powerful and comforting. This perspective contains a lot more power than that of feeling terrorized by God.

Reflection and Action

- Have you ever prayed from this perspective? If so, was it out of a need for comfort and reassurance or out of a fear of punishment (two very different things)?

- Consider ways to strengthen your belief in your own power to create change in your life. Identify times when it may be helpful to pray from a place of vulnerability, perhaps in search of solace and comfort.

Make me rich and successful. Give me things.

This prayer perspective tends to treat God as a kind of Santa Claus whose role is to deliver an endless supply of goods and riches. As a child, I often prayed to God to bring me wonderful toys and presents at Christmas. As I grew older, I prayed to God to help me do well in a baseball game or a track meet. I even remember praying to God to help me get a date with a particular girl. Prayers from this perspective can even take the form of bargaining or even wheeling and dealing. I made all kinds of deals and promises if only God would answer my prayers. In fact, I became quite good at bargaining with God.

This prayer perspective arises primarily out of a perceived lack of abundance, whether real or imagined, and is often driven by an ambitious need for success beyond all other priorities. If we look more closely at what underlies this intense desire to win, it is mostly the fear of not having enough. We all relate to this feeling at some point in our lives, and our contemporary society tends to emphasize material wealth as the standard of success in life over any other measurement, which masks our true desire: to be loved.

The spiritual assumption attached to prayers of intense ambition and greed is that, if you become rich, it means that God has favored you and that you deserve more, even when that abundance comes at the expense of others. And, of course, the inverse assumption is that, if you are poor, it means that God has not favored you and that no one else needs to help or support you because you have only yourself to blame for your misfortune.

Of course, we may be praying to God from a perspective of real physical need for resources such as adequate housing and food. In addition, at times we all have the desire for success in our endeavors or perhaps the desire to be more patient, generous, kind, and forgiving. Prayers that cry out to God to help with everyday physical needs or real problems like addictions, anxiety, and depression are of a totally different order than those motivated by greed.

From a shamanic point of view, prayers motivated by greed and ambition overemphasize the acquisition of material goods—of things and stuff—and this can turn prayer into a bargaining process. Our physical needs do absolutely need to be met. But the toys, fancy cars, huge houses, and wealth we seek are impermanent and ultimately unsatisfying. And sometimes these signs of material success can even cause problems. The admonition: "Be careful what you pray for; you might just get it," applies to this perspective.

Reflection and Action

- Have you ever prayed from this perspective? If so, was it out of physical need or actual want? Do you pray out of a sense of abundance, or out of a sense of lack? What does it mean to have "enough" in your life?

- Consider changing your prayers of request to prayers of gratitude; thanking Spirit for providing for you, for those things that are already yours. This shifts your position from one of lack to one of power.

Life is so hard! Why don't you help me?

This prayer perspective flows from anger and frustration with God—something that has been interwoven through art, ritual, and prayer throughout human history. Life can be hard and complicated, and it can certainly be filled with pain. Even those who seem outwardly successful or wealthy—those who seem to possess all that they could possibly want—may not have peace of mind, serenity, or tranquility.

When I was younger, I was sometimes so frustrated by praying to God without results that I railed in anger and felt totally martyred. Why did God seem to help other people, but not me? I enumerated all the extra things I did to make myself more deserving, but to no avail. God seemed silent and distant, or perhaps not there at all. I resented it when my prayers went unanswered.

There is so much stress and anxiety in the world that prayer from this perspective may become a mix of pleading, despair, and disbelief. It may include angry questions like: "Where are you?" "Why don't you help me?" "Why do you inflict so much suffering on this world?" "Why do bad things happen to good people?" "Why do the bad guys seem to have all the luck?" These are all powerful spiritual questions that have engaged countless philosophers, theologians, and spiritual leaders for thousands of years.

But praying solely from a place of helpless anger does not generate much power, shamanically speaking. The distress, fear, and emotion inherent in this style of prayer can rob it of its effectiveness and contribute greatly to feelings of limitation and negativity.

And this can result in disagreeable feelings of resentment.

As always, we can use these feelings as a springboard to rise to a higher level, move away from a position of victimization, and take responsibility for positive action in our lives. In this way we can transform this prayer perspective to focus on helping others. There is merit in working through your own beliefs about God's role in a world filled with injustice. We need to ask ourselves, does Spirit actually dole out pain and suffering, or does Spirit instead offer us the freedom to experience the consequences of our actions? Consider that if the answer to this question is the latter, then we have actually been given a great gift: the gift of choice. A healthy sense of balance is a key factor in this prayer perspective.

Reflection and Action

- Have you ever been angry at God in prayer? If so, what did it feel like to pray from that anger? Was it cleansing and cathartic, or did it only amplify your negativity? Were you angry because you weren't getting something you felt you deserved? Or because you felt that life is totally unfair and it's God's fault?

- Consider what you see as the role of God in a world where bad things happen to good people. Find ways to use your anger at injustice or unfairness in our society to fuel constructive and compassionate action, either for yourself or for others. Pray for the wisdom to see that there is always a bigger picture and that what seems unjust may have a deeper purpose that we do not yet understand.

Thank you for providing for me. I love you!

From the shamanic perspective, this fifth prayer perspective is the beginning of real power—power that arises out of a growing, all-encompassing sense that being alive is an extraordinary gift. As I grew older, I occasionally broke through my resentment and felt genuine gratitude for the chances and opportunities that came my way in life. I recovered some of the awareness and joy I had felt as a small child. My heart opened, and I realized that I had indeed been blessed. And I acknowledged that my life was, in fact, an extraordinary gift of freedom and opportunity.

This prayer perspective embraces an awareness that we did not create ourselves, but were instead created by a God who gave us the opportunity to be awake, to be aware, and to be conscious. This is an extraordinary miracle for which we should give thanks over and over in a state of awe and wonderment. It causes our hearts to open and pour out love to the great Provider and Creator of the whole Universe. It acknowledges the gifts that have already been given. From this perspective, there is no gulf between the one who prays and the One who receives that prayer.

Reflection and Action

- Have you ever felt an awareness of having been created? Have you ever acknowledged that life is a gift for which you are endlessly thankful? What words could you use to pray from this perspective?

- If you haven't felt this overwhelming sense of gratitude, consider ways you can purposefully cultivate this perspective in your life—gratitude journaling, volunteering, communing with nature, etc. If you have started to feel this sense of thanksgiving, find ways to share it with others.

Thank you for creating me. May the will of Spirit and my personal will be aligned.

To a shaman, this sixth prayer perspective is truly powerful. It is associated with real maturity—the perspective of someone who is a veteran of life. It is only recently that I have become reacquainted with the powerful God experiences I had in my early child-hood—the miracle of the awareness of being alive and conscious moment by moment. Spirit has shown me that, in my heart, I can find the Source of the life force and the doorway to all potential and all Creation.

This perspective is also characterized by gratitude and a recognition that the Source lies in the heart. The Creator is distributed into every particle of our bodies and makes up the life force that provides consciousness and awareness to everyone. God is not "out there," but "in here." There is no separation between us and the Creator and Provider of everything. From this perspective, we experience an eagerness to know God more and more and an accelerated awareness of the presence of God everywhere.

Prayer from this perspective acknowledges the connection, the communication within, the actualization of the energy of Source into everyday living. For the shaman, these prayers are about decreeing how it *is*. When you pray from this perspective, you realize that you are supplied by God moment by moment—that God is "dreaming you up" thousands of times a second and that you are truly made of "God stuff." You are God's eyes and ears; you are a reflection of Source; you are a projection of a tiny part of God into the physical world. And you are present in that world to explore and create in God's name.

Prayers from this perspective reinforce our connection to Spirit and recognize the huge responsibility we have as beings empowered by God to be mini-creators who, like God, create reality moment by moment. These prayers assert that God's will and my will have become one, so it is not a question of becoming a slave to God's will or insisting on my own individual will, but discovering instead that there is *no difference* between what I want and what Spirit wants of me. These prayers recognize that it is utterly futile to resist Spirit and that there is only Spirit working through everything. From this perspective, we can enjoy the Universe that Spirit has created through the expression of all things including me. From this perspective, we can affirm: "Spirit, through you I am healed." "Spirit, expand and sustain my success and happiness." "Spirit, may all beings be illuminated with the light of peace." This truly is the realm of the shaman.

Reflection and Action

- Have you ever felt that God lives in you and not just around you? What words can you use in a prayer from this perspective? How can you begin to cultivate this perspective in your life more purposefully? Do you personally know others who seem to radiate this perspective and who might be willing to mentor you for a time?

- Consider how this growing awareness of yourself as a cocreator in life influences, not only your prayer life, but also your day-to-day interactions with others, your work, and your purpose for being.

You and I are one. I Am.

This final perspective is difficult to speak about, because it transcends words. It is the powerful recognition that occurs during meditation and while contemplating the nature of reality. These prayers are for advanced practitioners and correspond to the maturity of an elder who has become a Master late in life. This maturity is well worth striving for no matter what your age, however, because its benefits and results are so profound.

Prayers from this perspective are more like experiences than verbal statements. This type of prayer asserts that Creator and self are one. There is no "other"—no separation, no duality—only integration and wholeness. When you pray from this perspective, you assert that God is a state of being and that all suffering is a product of the illusions that people project in their ignorance of Spirit. When this ignorance is banished in the light of consciousness, you recognize that there never was separation, never truly a banishment from the Garden of Eden, so to speak. God is; *I Am. I Am* the Word. May it be so.

Reflection and Action

- From this perspective, all questions seem to evaporate in favor of an expansive sense of peace.

Mixed Perspectives

If you found some of the previous section difficult to understand, that lack of understanding may be a function of where you are on your journey. For example, if you are praying from the first perspective—the perspective of survival—you may find it difficult to understand prayer from a more advanced perspective. Indeed, it's often the case that we can only understand prayers from those perspectives we have already experienced. A person who is praying from the fifth perspective, for example, may be able to understand the points of view of all the perspectives prior, but not of the perspectives that follow. This has led to grave misunderstandings about how to pray all over the world. For instance, some may regard prayers from the sixth perspective as sacrilegious, blasphemous, or heretical if they have only attained the second or third perspective.

We all experience moments of stress at different times in our lives. And these moments may invite prayer from perspectives that surprise us. Certainly fear, deprivation, and pain are actual human hardships that may prompt prayers of supplication or anger, or even a desire to triumph over adversaries—either fellow human beings or abstract concepts like poverty or depression. Yet, life invites us to constantly work toward a higher perspective. It's not bad that we have these hard feelings on occasion, but we should not allow ourselves to become trapped there.

In the chapters that follow, we will concentrate on prayers from the fifth, sixth, and possibly seventh perspectives because, from a shamanic standpoint, prayers from these perspectives are the ones that have the greatest power to make a difference. It makes sense for a helpless victim to offer a prayer of pleading, but this can sometimes have the effect of reinforcing helplessness and victimization. As a child asking for presents, you can only hope that you have been good enough and that an outside force will bring them. As an angry, confused, and suffering being, you can only hope for relief from an outside force. But when you acknowledge that you are connected to Spirit at the deepest levels, you gain access to the greatest powers of the Universe.

The minute gratitude enters your consciousness, you are on the shaman's path. On the one hand, the Creator requires no thanks, no worship, no acknowledgment. Think about it. A perfect being makes no demands. Yet gratitude is a powerful step on the path to recognition, because it opens our hearts to God and that reduces our sense of separation.

The more you assert your connection to the Creator, the more powerful you become. When you can see no more separation between self and Creator, all power becomes available to you. This is not sacrilege or heresy; it is the truth that all the great saints have discovered.

Chapter 3

Three Keys to Effective Prayer

The Holy Land is Everywhere.

—Black Elk

About four years ago, I had the good fortune to meet Beautiful Painted Arrow (Joseph Rael) and visit him at this home in southern Colorado. Rael had been selected by the Society for Shamanic Practice to receive the Eagle Feather Award for major contributions to the world of shamanism, and I had the honor to present him with the award and interview him for a podcast. Although he was in his early eighties, he was vibrant and sharp and took pleasure in sharing many of his extraordinary paintings and insights with me, including a number of them about prayer.

Rael is a Ute/Picuris chief and mystic, clearly an older soul, who has an extraordinary wealth of knowledge about the nature of reality. I had come across his writings some twenty years before, when I discovered his book *Being and Vibration*. He taught me about the power of sounds, the vibration of language, and the relationship of sound to the medicine wheel and all of reality. The vowels, he said, reveal the power in the Universe, while the consonants conduct that power to manifest ideas into physical form. He said that each vowel relates to a direction of the medicine wheel and is associated with a specific theme. Thus the words we choose to use in our prayers matter deeply.

Rael insisted on the Spanish pronunciation of vowels rather than the English, claiming that the vibrations of the vowel sounds in Spanish were closer to the actual physical makeup and shapes of our world. Thus the vowels related to the following positions and meanings on the medicine wheel:

A-Ahhh (East)—the vibration of purification

E-ehh (South)—the vibration of relationship

I-eee (West)—the vibration of awareness

O-ohhh (North)—the vibration of innocence

U-uuh (no direction)—the vibration of carrying

The words *I am* contain several vowel sounds. The sound of the letter *I* is made up of the vowels *A* and *E*, and thus relates to purification, relationship, and awareness. The pronoun *I* therefore means "pure awareness." The word *am* contains the vowel sound "Eh," signifying relationship, and the consonant sound "M," which directs a relationship with Spirit to create. When we say *I Am*, we are therefore saying: "Spirit creating pure awareness." This way of understanding sound and vibration in language completely changed my outlook on how words manifest ideas into physical reality.

The Powerful and Essential *I Am*

It was not until I remembered the importance that the words *I am alive* had for me in my earliest childhood that my prayers become truly powerful. Because of my many years studying Eastern philosophy, I was under the impression that the word *I* signified the ego, false personality, or self-importance and should be avoided. Little did I know that, because of this, my prayers had been missing the mark and were lacking the key to open my heart. But when I learned that the word *I* refers rather to Essence, I understood its value. *I* is a shared concept that refers to all human beings as pure awareness coexisting in the state of *I Am*.

I and *am* are thus the two most powerful words we can ever utter. They are the formative words of Creation that align us with Spirit better than almost anything else we can say or do. Just thinking the phrase *I Am* invokes the universal life force given to us by Spirit—that energy that keeps us alive moment by moment. A singer once told me that, before every major performance, he experienced terrible stage fright. To help himself calm down, he repeated the phrase *I Am* over and over to himself. This invariably brought him to a peaceful state, so that, when he went on stage, he sang from his soul and his performances were magical.

I Am references our total uniqueness as created beings. It expresses individualized consciousness or conscious awareness, the place from which we each cocreate with Spirit. Paradoxically, although the words are utterly personal, they also refer to the *I Am* in everything and are thus synonymous with Essence. Each human being has an Essence that is the sum total of who they have been, who they are in the moment, and how they show up. This Essence, sometimes called soul, is the source of each person's life. It is created by Spirit and makes up each person's link to the Creator.

All vowel sounds can be used as significant mantras, special sounds that open up specific areas of awareness. The "Ahhh" sound appears in other important spiritual words like *Amen, Allah, Yahweh,* and *Aum.* The sound of the word *Am* opens doors or energetic pathways to the infinite. You will have to experience this to understand it.

In his most powerful teachings, the great shaman Jesus, who always taught by example, used these words with great deliberation—"*I Am* that I am." "*I Am* the resurrection and the light." "*I Am* the light of the world." Like so many great spiritual teachers, he referred to meditation and prayer as the path to redemption—"If your eye be single, your body will be filled with light." Here he refers to the process of turning the eyes upward and inward and focusing deeply into the third ventricle of the brain, the location that Tibetans call the Crystal Palace and Huichols call the Mansion. (We will discuss this concept in more depth in the next chapter.)

It is no accident that the sound of the English vowel *I* is also the sound of the word *eye*, which is sometimes considered as the doorway to the soul. Both words, both sounds, evoke the same thing—light. The location on the forehead sometimes called the Third Eye is the place from which we perceive the true *I*—not the ego, but Spirit. Similarly, as we will discuss in a later chapter, this All-Seeing Eye (also called the Mansion) represents a powerful path to enlightenment for the Toltecs. It is also worth noting here that the word *shaman* means "one who sees in the dark."

It is important when praying to use the phrase *I Am* frequently, but never ever with a negative connotation or to refer to any difficulty. Negatives should only be expressed in the past tense, as things or feelings that are already behind you. *I Am* should only be used to express positive thoughts. The phrase can also be used in group prayer to express "us" or "we." *I Am* is more accurate in this case, however, because there is truly only One behind the many. Whenever you come across this phrase, in whatever context, remember to feel it deep in your heart and to remind yourself of its power.

The Alchemical Power of *What–If*

Children love to play what-if. What if I were Batman? What if you were Wonder Woman? What if a big monster came out of that old house over there? What if we were twenty feet tall? This tried-and-true question unleashes the creative imaginations of children everywhere. When we are older, we still play what-if? But we play it in more negative ways. "What if I can't pay my taxes this year?" "What if I get sick?" "What if our house loses value?" Unfortunately, adult what-ifs are often coopted by our worries and concerns and help to instill fear.

But we also use the question when we are imagining more productive situations. "What if we put the house on that end of the lot?" "What if I paint the bedroom blue?" "What if I bought some shares of this successful company?" "What if we bought that old house, fixed it up, and resold it for a big profit?" "What if we added this valve-closure system to the artificial heart?" "What if we tried this asthma medication for that dermatitis condition?" All these what-ifs are based in curiosity, and curiosity is a major path to invention, evolution, and development. These what-if questions can lead us to experimentation that eventually leads us to life-changing breakthroughs.

There are two reasons why this works. First, what-if questions don't prompt any resistance in our minds; they are just a way in which we wonder about things. Second, what-if questions engage our imaginations and our imaginations, are critical to producing the results we desire.

What-if questions thus give us an opportunity to bring together the power of prayer and the power of curiosity, vivid imagination, and intention to achieve a desired result. This combination can be extremely potent, because it allows us to engage with our prayer in a proactive way that elicits the ancient alchemical powers of creation. In effect, it helps us to answer our own prayers without even realizing it. Yet we need even more than this powerful tool to get the most from our prayers.

Completing the Circuit

The final and magical key to effective prayer is, simply put, completing the circuit with Spirit. There is a tiny port inside the human heart to which Essence connects, just like the connection between your computer and the wall socket from which it draws its power. Essence, or Spirit, animates much of the physical body in a similar way when we connect to it through this tiny little spot in our hearts. Through this connection, we draw the power that activates our aliveness and awareness and provides life to our bodies. This power source, connected through this tiny port, is active twenty-four hours a day from the moment of our birth to the moment of our death.

Many years of my life had passed before I discovered this ultimate key to prayer. Like so many truths, it was right in front of me all along, but I didn't really grasp it or understand it. Once my shaman teachers opened my mind so that I could begin to see hints in my own prayers, however, I finally awakened one day to a great "aha!" experience.

I have discovered that, when I fix my attention on this spot in my heart, I always feel good. That's why I call it the "glad-to-be-alive spot." To get a rough sense of where it lies, find the sensitive spot in the center of your sternum and press lightly. This is the sinoatrial node, which is located just behind and to the left of the top right side of your heart. Physiologically, this structure is responsible for creating the electrical impulses that enable the beating of a healthy heart. From this spot, Spirit pours out a constant stream of intelligence and life force that gives us the pure blessing and gift of light. The Toltecs call this the "place of flowering" because like flowers, we are all moving toward our greatest blossoming. No wonder shamanism is called the path with heart!

The secret to successful prayer lies in completing a spiritual circuit that returns our attention back to this sacred spot in our hearts. We can achieve this by focusing our intent there and using the mantras *I Am* and *What if.* This combination of intent and affirmation opens the door to the heart. By directing our awareness, our gratitude, and our love back to the place in our hearts where Essence dwells, we complete that circuit and connect with Spirit or God. And this is how our prayers and decrees attain their full dynamic power.

Many great spiritual teachers have told us that the entrance to heaven is through an open heart. Shamans and mystics the world over say it requires an open heart to enter the world of Spirit where the Source of all things lies. In fact, shamans and other mystics use drums during ceremony and prayer precisly because they mimic the heartbeat.

To pray effectively, you must direct your attention to this source of power in your heart, while reciting *I Am* or asking *What if*. Once you feel the buzz of life there, you are ready to pray. From a shaman's point of view, prayers offer directions about what you want Spirit to do and confirm your awareness of your connection to Spirit. "Spirit, thanks to you I am enjoying perfect health and happiness!" "Spirit, I am thankful that I am filled with your love and prosperity!" "Spirit, take charge of my thoughts and feelings, and erase all negativity and doubt." "Spirit, guide me to manifest myself as healthy, wealthy, and wise."

But prayers can also act as questions that can help you acknowledge and utilize the power of Spirit. "What if I receive the clearest most dynamic response from Spirit that I have ever had?" "What if my prayers are answered beyond my wildest expectations?" "What if I were to know exactly what to do and exactly when I should do it?" Offered from a positive perspective, these prayers can be remarkably effective as well.

In the next chapter, we'll explore how to prepare our spaces and ourselves so that our prayers can be most effective.

Chapter 4

Preparing for Prayer

May the stars carry your sadness away. May the flowers fill
your heart with beauty. May hope forever wipe away your
tears, and above all, may silence make you strong.
—Chief Dan George

There are literally thousands of ways in which people around the world prepare for prayer. These include fasting and dieting with plants, like the Shipibo and other indigenous tribes; doing chi gong, a millennia-old system of coordinated posture, movement, and breathing; performing meditation and mudras; bathing with oils; and communing with nature. I like to use the Huichol Mansion practice (explained below) and Toltec breathing practices to bring in energy and power before praying. I also like to greet the sun prior to praying or pray while bathing in the light of the sunrise or sunset. While there is no "right way" to prepare to pray, there are methods that I have found produce much stronger results, and I will share these with you here.

Life is complicated and, sometimes, you may have to skip any preparations before you pray, especially if you are saying a spontaneous prayer for something in the moment. But setting aside a specific time each day for prayer—for example, early morning or before sleep—can make all the difference in how effective your prayers will be by including your preparations as part of your routine. When you set aside time to prepare for and engage in prayer on a regular basis, it can have a big impact. As always, the proof is in the pudding.

Mantras

I like to begin my prayers with short phrases or mantras that are actually prayers in and of themselves. These function as energy regulators or attunements that harmonize me with higher octaves and states of consciousness. You can use these alchemical formulas to transform your state of awareness from ordinary to transcendent. Since problems cannot be solved at the level or vibration in which they were created, the only solution is to raise the level of vibration. Then solutions and changes appear as if by magic.

Here are some phrases that are very powerful. Be mindful and respectful when you use them.

All is sacred, as am I.

All is holy, as am I.

All is divine, as am I.

All is blessed, as am I.

All is filled with love, as am I.

I have also worked with phrases like these:

I Am known by Spirit, who is everywhere.

I Am known by the sacred all around me.

The divine smile knows me and approves of me.

The all-knowing eye sees me and transforms me.

I know who *I Am* in Truth and Love.

I Am aware of my awareness.

I have come to the upper room (mansion).

I see you in the upper room.

I know who I am in truth and love.

I make all things new.

The sky is the limit with phrases like these. Use them as an inspiration for creating your own similar mantras. The only thing that matters is that your mantras be uplifting, that they feel expansive to you, and that they make you feel good. If you find yourself feeling guilty while repeating them—perhaps because they appear foreign or unfamiliar to you or seem somehow narcissistic or grandiose—simply breathe with intention and work to let these feelings go. They come from your ego, which always tries to keep you from knowing your true nature. The ego might prefer phrases like: "All is miserable, as am I" or "All is ugly, as am I." But those phrases would, of course, be lies.

Be careful not to utter these mantras in a rote way or in a state of distraction. Pay attention to what you are saying and allow yourself to feel the emotion bubbling up within you as you voice each phrase. Notice the enormity of what each phrase means, the purity of the truth within it. Allow yourself to experience your own grand nature and the grandness of all of Spirit's creations. Ask yourself how anything can exist outside of Spirit if Spirit is everywhere and infinite. Then contemplate how you participate in this larger existence.

The mantras given above make excellent prayers and harmonizers. They can be effective when used all by themselves as stand-alone rituals, even for as short a time as thirty seconds. They can totally transform your life for the better. And this is what lies at the heart of the shamanic Toltec way, the path of the ancient Mexicas.

Opening the Fields

Another method I like to use to prepare for prayer is a practice I call "opening the fields." We have seen that words carry vibrations. Every word in every language represents a certain vital experience that is expressed as a vibration. *Cloud* is a vibration. *Tree* is a vibration. *Mountain* is a vibration. *Forgiveness* is a vibration, as are *generosity* and *kindness*. These vibrations overlap and occupy the same space all around us and within us. They function exactly like the many radio, television, and Internet channels that are broadcast around the globe without our even noticing them unless we turn on a radio or a television that can receive them. Even though these broadcasts are always "on," so to speak, we may not benefit from them because we may forget to tune in to them.

The way to tune in to these vibrations is simply to name them and allow yourself to be open to them—"opening the fields." You can attune yourself to these vibrations and make them part of your awareness using phrases like: "Open the field of clarity." "Open the field of beauty." "Open the fields of generosity, kindness, and compassion." "Open the fields of wisdom, expansiveness, and fulfillment." "Open the fields of unconditional love, abundance, and creativity." "Open the fields of miracles, healing, and wholeness." You get the idea. You can open any field or set of fields whenever you choose. Now, you may be thinking that it can't possibly be that easy or that it will never work. All I can say is: Try it and see what happens.

In the mystic traditions and from a shamanic perspective, your word is law in the Universe. You can therefore use your words for either good or ill. You will get better at this with practice, so give it a chance and look for even the slightest evidence that it is working. For the practice to work, however, you have to believe in it and give it time. Your success will grow from there. In fact, this practice can be a complete and extremely powerful prayer all by itself. And it works even better when you follow it up with other prayers.

Obviously, you will want to open fields that make you feel good, rather than fields that do not. For example, it would be pointless to open up the fields of anxiety, depression, rage, shame, or guilt. Why would you do that? But too often, we open these vibrational fields without realizing it. It's probably a good idea to check in with yourself before your prayer time to become aware of the state your mind is in. If you are not in a good state of mind before praying, try closing off fields that don't make you feel good. You can do this simply by using command like these: "Close the field of depression." "Close the field of anxiety."

"Close the field of discouragement." Then open the fields that you would rather have open. Curiously, the more you open certain fields, the more they will stay open, just as certain neurological pathways in your brain grow with repeated use.

Your consciousness is a part of the larger consciousness of the physical Universe that is evolving and growing bit by bit over vast stretches of time. This consciousness begins to accelerate when it evolves into individualized self-aware beings like ourselves. According to numerous shamanic prophecies from tribes like the Hopi, the Maya, the Tibetans, and the Toltecs, this is a critical time in history in which we are taking a quantum leap in consciousness. These prayers and phrases are the technology that can help make this happen. Please take advantage of them and make liberal use of them.

Entering the Mansion

Many traditions say that there is a space—a command post, if you will—in your brain that is key to praying with power. This space has been known to mystics, shamans, and great saints of various traditions for thousands of years. It has been called by many names in many different cultures and in many different languages. Huichols call it the Mansion; Shipibos call it El Templo (the temple); Hindus call it the Cave of Brahma; Tibetans call it the Crystal Palace; medical professionals and neurologists call it the third ventricle of the brain.

There are four ventricles in your brain and they are all connected like a cave system. The first and second ventricles are lateral to the third ventricle in the center. This third ventricle is the one we will be working with. The fourth is below and behind the third ventricle, on the brain stem. These ventricles together, when seen from a shamanic perspective, look like an eagle in flight. The third ventricle would be the head and body of the bird, the first and second ventricles the wings in flight, and the fourth would be the feet hanging down. This is not accidental according to shamanic understanding. This bird would be seen as an ally.

Biologically speaking, the third ventricle is located in the exact center of the brain between the pituitary gland, the pineal gland, the thalamus, and the hypothalamus. It is filled with cerebrospinal fluid and acts to prevent trauma to the brain. It, like all the ventricles, functions as a channel through which the cerebrospinal fluid can flow as it brings in nutrients and carries off waste from the brain. In an esoteric sense, it can be likened to the bridge on a ship from which the captain steers and issues commands. To mystics and shamans, it is a sacred and powerful place

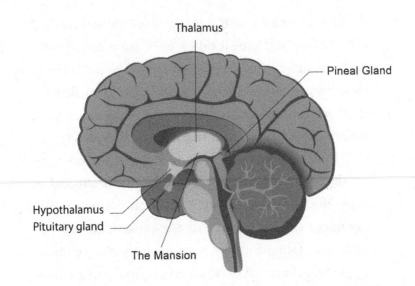

Thalamus

Pineal Gland

Hypothalamus

Pituitary gland

The Mansion

that is capable of holding extremely high vibrations and generating powerful fields of energy around the head and upper body.

By itself, this ventricle does not do anything beyond fulfilling its biological functions. But many shamans see it as the portal to the world of Spirit—a liminal space where we can access the blueprints of all things past, present, and future outside of time and space. Moreover, there are ways to wake it up, activate it, and open its higher octaves so that it can perform many more functions than those recognized by biologists or the medical profession.

Here are some simple steps that can help you enter the Mansion and turn it on or wake it up. To locate this spot, draw a line from your Third Eye (between your brows) to the back of your head. Then draw another line that connects the tips of your ears. The third ventricle lies at the intersection of these lines.

Now focus your attention on this spot and imagine that there is a golden egg standing vertically and filling the space, with its fatter end on the bottom and its thinner end on top. Set that egg spinning counterclockwise, facing forward, with the back part of the egg moving from left to right and the front part moving from right to left. Let the spinning motion settle into a speed that feels natural and right to you—most likely faster rather than slower. Sense the egg beginning to generate a scalar wave, a golden light that extends throughout your head and beyond—all the way to just below your heart and outward to form a perfectly round globe around your head.

Take a moment to sense this light and feel how it is impacting you. In my experience, this begins as a subtle sensation that grows in intensity the more often you do the exercise. Feel the instantaneously calming effect the light has on you and let yourself enjoy the serene and tranquil state of mind it produces. My students have told me that their experience of this light is one of ecstasy and wonder. And there is a good reason for this. The light is incompatible with fear. When you are immersed in its glow, you literally cannot experience states of fear. If you do feel fear, this tells you that you have not yet entered the Mansion or that you have only succeeded in entering it for a few moments. You just need more practice. When you sense the light and its effects, you will know that you have activated the Mansion and caused the portal located there to open to a high vibrational space or landscape.

This golden glow has been portrayed by many medieval artists as a halo around great saints' heads. Jesus, the Buddha, Krishna, Mother Mary, the twelve apostles, Mary Magdalene, Quan Yin, and other great teachers have all been depicted with halos around their heads. You can find many of these images on the Internet. This halo of light indicates that their Mansions had been activated and their portals opened. Some of them may have used the technique given here, while others may have had a spontaneous or revelatory experience.

This method for entering the Mansion provides a very easy and effective preparation for prayer. With practice, you will be able to activate this light in a matter of a few seconds. Eventually, if you are ready, it will remain available to you permanently. Be aware, however, that, if you activate this light using the spinning egg technique, you must prepare yourself for some consequences. Just as when you fast, you may feel some initial discomfort, because the generation of the light can trigger egoic resistance as you vibrate loose old blockages. This simply means that you have confronted the ego and are getting rid of whatever may be blocking your access to higher octaves. Think about how sore your muscles feel after you work out. It may not be pleasant, but it's a good sign that you are getting into shape.

Physical Postures

According to shamans everywhere, certain postures and positions constitute prayers without words. One ancient Toltec prayer position places the shaman facing the rising sun at dawn with his legs shoulder-width apart and his knees bent. Gradually arching his back, shoulders, and head forward, and turning his face up toward the sun, he then lifts his arms up and stretches them out to either side until they are horizontal with his shoulders, with his hands facing the sun and his fingers outstretched in what is called the "great wings position."

This traditional posture is a prayer of complete surrender to Spirit. In it, the heart becomes completely vulnerable and is offered symbolically to Spirit and focused toward the sun. An imaginary arrow is loosed from the heart directly into the sun to connect with it and to indicate great gratitude for its light, warmth, and life-giving energy. The shaman then makes requests. After a minute or so, he relaxes his body, lowers his arms, and straightens his back, returning to a normal standing position. This ritual is repeated three times. Eventually, the ritual use of this posture spread northward from Mexico and was adopted by the Lakota Sioux as part of their Sacred Sundance ceremony.

There are many such postures, each with its own meaning. You can choose from a variety of them to use while praying. Some of them allow you to pray anywhere—in your car, in an elevator, in the bathroom, on an airplane, or walking down a crowded urban street. There is no right place or right way to use them. Just do what feels right and natural for you.

I spent many years of my childhood on my knees praying on a hard wooden floor or on a kneeler in church, so I tend to avoid kneeling at this point in my life. You, on the other hand, may find yourself best prepared for prayer when you are in a kneeling position. Just do what feels natural. I have never seen a shaman pray on his knees. But if you like kneeling, by all means kneel.

Chapter 5

Manifesting Through Prayer

As you walk upon the sacred earth,
treat each step as a prayer.
—Black Elk

Twenty-five years ago, I was invited down to the Peruvian Amazon by a Frenchman who had been living with the Shipibo for a number of years. He functioned as a medic for a time and eventually adopted the tribe's ceremonial and shamanic healing practices, finding them more effective than most of the allopathic medicine in which he had been trained. Ultimately, he became an *ayahuasqero*, a shaman who uses the ayahuasca vine to heal. Because he was an excellent botanist, he also explored other powerful plant medicines and dieting practices used by the Shipibo.

It was when I went down to a remote part of the upper Amazon jungle in Peru to participate in a challenging tobacco diet that I met the Shipibo for the first time and learned of their powerful manifesting practices. These practices used the plants of the jungle, the songs (*icaros*) of the plants, and handwoven textiles decorated with designs depicting plant *icaros* to empower their rituals. This alien world proved to have a profound influence on my life. Since then, during over forty trips to Peru, I have learned a great deal about dieting with plants, performing their *icaros*, and using the sacred textiles that are based on these songs. In the course of this long training, I learned how the Shipibo used the ayahuasca vine to heal and ultimately became an *ayahuasqero* myself.

The Shipibo taught me that each plant has a unique song and unique gifts that can help us unlock its powers. Some plants give abundance, some heal wounds and illnesses, some assist in difficult relationships, some support business negotiations, some erase fear and build confidence, and some relax the body and open the mind to powerful truths through visions. In short, their gifts help us to manifest our dreams, our hopes, and our desires, but only if they are honored, if their songs are sung, and if the power of focus and intention is applied. This knowledge has transformed my life for the better.

The work of an *ayahuasqero* is all about manifesting ideas into reality. The *icaros,* or sacred songs, of the plants are all forms of prayer that relate to their medicinal properties. Some are ancient and traditional, but new songs are always being "grabbed out of the air," so to speak, and given voice. Singing these songs provides a rich and powerful way to pray, especially when singing for someone else's benefit or healing. Each song is associated with a design that can be woven into cloth or painted on clothing, walls, and canvases. Sometimes temporary tattoos for protection, healing, good fishing, healthy crops, or other matters are created from these designs.

One of the primary purposes of prayer is to manifest goals, states, and conditions more deliberately. This can be done through singing, chanting, or simply speaking. We often pray because we desire to transform our lives. We may want to change conditions like hardship, poverty, or the pain of loss. We may want to draw improved conditions like success, love, and abundance toward us. That's just human nature. We all want to be more prosperous, no matter what our station in life. Some may not want to admit it, but we all want to have more opportunity, more success, more influence, more resources, or more talent in our lives. And there is absolutely nothing wrong with these aspirations. After all, the more resources we have at our disposal, the more good we can do in the world.

Although we may hope for miracles, it is our prayers that actually bring about these transformations when they are constructed in a special way. In fact, shamans say that we are the creators of our lives. The Secoya tribe in Ecuador and Peru says that we are dreamers who dream our lives into manifestation. I believe this is true. Our purpose as human beings is both to experience life and to learn to mold the primary components of reality according to our desires. This is also one of the ultimate goals of the shamanic path.

Four important elements contribute to our being able to manifest our desires through shamanic prayer. All burgeoning creators must master these elements. They are attention, intent, feeling, and envisioning.

Attention

Your life is shaped by where you place your attention. Attention is, in fact, critical to creating. Your attention compels life to flow wherever you place it. When you turn your attention to something negative, you give it the power to limit you. You must learn to focus instead on your Essence and its connection to Spirit.

Your attention often reflects your deepest desires. If those desires are positive and you can stay focused on them, you will likely be able to manifest your positive dreams. But the opposite can also be true. If you focus your attention on negative desires, you are more likely to manifest those emotions—whether they be fear, guilt, or hatred.

Using your attention correctly requires tremendous discipline, but is well worth the effort. Your goal should be to fix your attention on what you want and avoid fixing it on what you don't want. This means developing the ability to focus your attention for long periods of time. This is a key element of manifesting through prayer.

Spiritual teachers throughout the ages have developed methods to accomplish this. But you can also control your attention using something you have with you all the time—your breath. In fact, one of the simplest way to develop your powers of attention is simply to watch your breath. Watch it as you inhale, hold your breath for three seconds, and watch it as you exhale. Repeat this as often as necessary, holding your breath for three seconds between each repetition. See how long you can focus on your breath without being distracted by other intruding thoughts. When these other thoughts arise, practice redirecting them and not being carried away by them. If this happens, just return to your breathing.

The thinking mind is a powerful force. If you feel it tugging at your attention, don't get upset with yourself. Just concentrate again on your breath.

Although this may sound simple, it is actually quite difficult to do. But the ability to discipline your attention is absolutely necessary for successful prayer.

Practice this breathing technique for five minutes each day and see if you can extend the time you attend to your breathing without giving in to intrusive thoughts. Then lengthen the practice as you become more accomplished at it. To clear your mind, try looking at a body of water or the sky and saying something like "clear sky" or "clear water." Or look at a spiritual icon, a picture, or a statue to keep your attention focused.

Because the present moment is the core of your experience, it is best to pray only for what you want in the present. And remember to pray as if what you want is already present in your life. Your prayers are weakened by words like: "I hope I will be able to," or "I will someday," or "Spirit, if you could see fit to."

Intent

Your intent defines where you choose to direct your attention. It is determined by what you choose to pray for. Intent is not mere wishing or hoping, but rather your expressed desire to manifest an outcome or create something new or different in your life. For a shaman, everything in life exists by intent, otherwise it wouldn't be there.

Intent implies certainty, the deep knowing that wherever you place your attention is real, valid, and true. Just think about some of the things of which you are already certain. Perhaps you are certain that you love someone. Consider how you know that and notice what it feels like. Perhaps you are certain that you are alive, or that you have eyes to see, or that you have shoes on your feet. Become aware of the feeling of absolute positive certainty that accompanies these thoughts, and carry this same feeling over to your prayers.

From the shamanic worldview, whatever you see in your life right now is what Essence intended. When you understand that Essence is cocreating your life with Spirit, you suddenly become free, because you can go about re-creating your life *consciously*. The first step is simply to accept that you have this power. The second is to intend something new. This is not as simple as it sounds, however, because, to hold an intention successfully, you must have absolute certainty that it will come to pass. In the meantime, your best bet is to practice having confidence in your intentions. Just "fake it until you make it."

Your heart is the center of your intent; it is where you have the most powerful connection to Essence. When you focus on your heart, you experience a constant certainty, as well as confidence and clarity. When you connect to Essence in your heart, you make a clear statement that it will direct your prayers and keep them powerfully focused.

Feeling

Feelings flow from where you place your attention. Most of the time, you feel good when you place your attention on Essence, on being connected to Spirit, on the *I Am* state. When you feel bad, it is most likely because your false personality, your ego, is paying attention to whatever is causing discord or separation in your life. When you feel good, you enjoy access to a tremendous source of power; when you feel bad, you fall prey to an enormous energy leak.

Feelings and thoughts are entwined in a tight embrace. Often feelings drive thoughts, and those thoughts can, in turn, drive more feelings. One key to creating powerfully is to direct your thoughts to those things that elicit positive feelings. These can then generate more positive feelings, and it will be easier for you to hold your attention on these things. This is a self-reinforcing endeavor, because when you develop your intent and direct your thoughts to produce positive feelings, you fulfill the desire that Essence has for you to feel good. In fact, Essence never feels bad and never wants you to feel bad. Only your ego does that. And that is where the work lies. Your self-important ego, your false personality, is constantly distracted by drama and external phenomena that are almost always connected to suffering and bad feelings. And it wants to drag you along with it. Ultimately, this can keep you from manifesting what you want through your prayers.

No one can become a master creator when their feelings are running amok. Learning to redirect your feelings when they fixate on something inharmonious or negative can be challenging. But it is a necessary practice. Unfortunately, life presents us with many negative conditions that we have a hard time avoiding. A simple glance at a newspaper or watching the television news illustrates this point. You cannot entirely avoid the negativity in the world all around you. The trick is to observe it without getting sucked into it and letting it ruin your day. You have to learn to acknowledge negative circumstances without rewarding them with your attention.

The key is to look at negative circumstances and say: "Oh, another mass shooting. People hurting each other. Too bad! I can't fix it and feeling bad about it does not help. Now, where was I? Oh yes, I was focusing on my vision for being of service in a more effective way." This may sound cold, ruthless, or callous, but it is nothing of the sort. You can experience these intense feelings, but choose rather to honor the constant intensity of your creative Source in your heart. To pray effectively, you must be able to direct your emotion. Otherwise, you leave yourself at the mercy of one disaster after another and become powerless. And you cannot afford to be powerless. Discipline is the only answer.

Envisioning

Envisioning means being able to see, sense, and feel what you pray about. From a shaman's point of view, we are each cocreators with Spirit. We create through our dreams, which are a combination of attention, intent, feeling, and envisioning. Taken together, these forces propel our dreams into physical reality.

Your prayers depend on your power to envision or know without words what you are praying about. For this, you need imagination, something everyone has, although it may work differently for different people. You will have to discover the best way to utilize your own imagination so you can see, sense, or feel what you are praying about.

The important point here is that just saying a bunch of words is useless. But saying words with attention, intent, feeling, and vision is powerful. The more you can incorporate your senses into your prayers, the better. This includes touching, smelling, seeing, hearing, and deeper senses like knowing or intuiting. I sing my prayers like the Huichol and

Shipibo because, as I sing, I can hear the music and the melody and that stirs up more emotion than I feel when I am simply speaking. Sometimes I whistle or hum or play a drum or rattle, because these all make my prayers more alive. You can also accompany your prayers with musical instruments like a guitar, a flute, or a harmonium—whatever you like. My mentor Guadalupe often accompanied his prayers with a little Huichol violin that lends an eerie but beautiful quality to prayers raised at night around a fire in the extraordinary Sonoran Desert.

Gathering and Storing Power

In order to manifest, you must generate the power to propel your intent through vision and into physical reality. Although we are each born with an ample supply of power, we tend to let it leak away through bad habits, worry, negative thinking, and a host of faulty behaviors. Eventually, we become depleted and wonder why we have such trouble manifesting anything. How can we plug these leaks so that we can gather and store more energy?

There are many methods for gathering and storing energy—some physical, some mental, and some emotional. Being out in nature is one of the most effective ways to gather and store energy physically. Studying how the Universe works builds power through understanding and knowledge. The Toltecs call their shamans "people of knowledge" because they study, learn, and gather knowledge about reality and the laws of the Universe. As you have seen, opening the heart and talking to Spirit—expressing gratitude, love, and awe—builds power through vibration and emotion. It is important to cultivate all three.

Your dreams have lesser or greater power to manifest depending on the power source you use. When you try to do everything alone, your power source is like a weak battery. The Toltecs tell us that there are greater sources of power that we can harness to drive our dreams and visions. They pull power from the sun and the moon as they pray, asking them to recognize their prayers and help them heal, resolve problems, and attract favorable circumstances. By plugging in to the great power source of Spirit through the sun and the moon, they harness them as allies to produce greater results. Likewise Taoists tell us to cultivate more chi to fuel our intent.

Shamans the world over greet the sun at sunrise and the moon at moonrise and direct prayers to them. They know that the sun and the moon are very powerful manifestations of Spirit and essential sources of power. Of course, they draw on other sources of power as well—crashing waves at the seashore, waterfalls, rainbows, great mountains, hot- or cold-water springs, caverns, canyons, storms, animal herds, great forests, and crystals. All these and more can become sources of fuel for prayers to manifest. Praying in the presence of the morning sun, the full moon, a vibrant rainbow, or tall trees can make your prayers much more powerful than praying at the side of your bed.

Four Steps to Manifestation

Manifesting your prayers is a process comprised of four steps: knowing your intention, claiming your desire, receiving your desire, and owning your desire. If you are confused, ambivalent, or doubtful about any of these steps, you likely will not get what you pray for. You can pray for clarification on any one of these steps, or you can pray for guidance and support to help you carry them out effectively. Prayer is always the solution. Prayer is always a way forward. Prayer is always a source of support.

Know Your Intention

In order to manifest the object of your prayers, you have to know what you are praying for or intending to bring in. Some think that the details of your desire or intention are important, but I believe you can leave the details to Spirit. In other words, Spirit knows best. As long as you can name your desire and understand and express it—better relationships, resources to travel to a specific destination, a mate, improved respiratory or digestive health, a promotion, acceptance to a program—you will succeed.

Claim Your Desire

Next you must be willing to claim your desire. A claim is a statement of expectation. When I make a claim— for example, when I claim my car after a nice meal at a restaurant that offers valet service—I expect it to be delivered to me. If I don't produce my claim check and make the claim, my car will not be delivered.

Receive Your Desire

You also have to be open to receiving your desire. If I order a new piece of furniture and have it delivered, I have to open the door for the delivery person or I will never receive it. That's quite clear.

Own Your Desire

And finally, you have to own your desire. Once the valet delivers my car to me, I must climb in and drive off in it. After all, it does belong to me.

Prayers for Manifesting

Here are some prayers that can help you focus your attention, clarify you intent, cultivate your feelings, and enable your visioning.

PRAYER TO ENHANCE POWER

The following prayer uses a Native American format. "A Ho" refers to either "Thank you" or "Amen," or may be used to indicate "All my relations" who are witnessing my prayers. I learned this simple prayer from a Native American woman, and then I put my own spin on it. You can use it to enhance all elements of shamanic prayer. Repeat it once for each element—attention, intent, feeling, and vision—while concentrating on that element. Then repeat it a fifth time to integrate all four elements into one powerful bid for manifestation. Here are five brief examples:

I Am experiencing harmony;
A Ho Spirit, make it so.

I Am experiencing love;
A Ho Spirit, make it so.

I Am experiencing vitality;
A Ho Spirit, make it so.

I Am experiencing inspiration;
A Ho Spirit, make it so.

I Am experiencing beauty;
A Ho Spirit, make it so.

As always, feel free to adapt the specific words of this prayer for your own needs. I've given five examples here, but you should feel free to add more if so moved. Sometimes a long, repeating prayer is called for to establish a rhythmic sense of timelessness and connection.

PRAYER TO ENHANCE INTENT

Spirit of Life, you intended for me to be here, and *I Am* here.

Spirit of Awakening, you intended for me to wake up, and *I Am* waking up.

Spirit of Being, you intended for me to create, and *I Am* creating this moment.

Let my intentions be enfolded within yours, arising from the same place,

Moving toward the same horizon.

Spirit, as the potter shapes the cup, *I Am* shaping my intention

To know you better,

To be fully present,

To be joyful,

To serve with gladness,

To be wise.

(Add your personal intentions here—there is no limit!)

Spirit, as the cup is filled with water, so may my heart be filled with purpose.

From this moment, may my intent be always and ever your intent.

Whatever blooms and manifests in the course of my life

Is what we have shaped together.

PRAYER TO ENHANCE CONNECTION

This prayer can help you build the power you will need to manifest your dreams quickly. You can combine this prayer with other methods like being out in nature or praying at a powerful place.

Great Spirit,

You are always in each moment creating every particle of every star,

Every blade of grass.

There is nothing as powerful as you are.

I Am grounding my being in the awareness of your power.

I Am conscious of it in every breath I take.

I Am opening the doors of my heart to this energy.

Every cell of my body is alive with light and vitality.

I Am rooted in the energy from the planet, which rises

Up through my feet and my spine and into my chest,

Flowing out of my arms and hands, through my throat,

And up the base of my skull.

I Am offering this vital energy out and up to the sky,

And the energy from the sky descends in blessing,

Flowing down into the top of my head, down into the
base of my spine.

Earth and Sky flow up and down my spine in a
continuous dance.

I Am utterly connected to all life—

Earth, air, fire, water;

Sun, moon, stars, wind;

Mountain, desert, sea.

Every atom of my body glows with exquisite light.

And this burning flame turns violet, radiating though
my body,

Collecting in and recharging the centers of
my strength—

Belly, heart, and Third Eye.

This is my birthright—

To manifest my dreams,

To create happiness and joy,

To create peace and prosperity,

To alleviate suffering.

Great Spirit, through our connection

I Am welcoming power;

I Am radiating power;

I Am holding power;

And *I Am* filled with gratitude.

May I always remember to use this power well,

With your guidance, to manifest your Great Dream.

PART TWO

PRAYERS FOR LIFE

Chapter 6

Prayers for Communing with Spirit

When you find tears in your eyes
you know you are truly praying.
—Guadalupe Candelario

The Toltecs of ancient Mexico taught that everything in manifest form came from the emanations of the Black Eagle and all of reality is kept in form by these very emanations. This includes all human beings, as well as everything we can see, sense, or feel. Once, in my early twenties, under the influence of a strong plant medicine, I saw these emanations everywhere I looked—even coming out of my own hands. When I looked in the mirror, I saw them coming out of all parts of me. And I saw them coming out of dogs and cats and all the people I saw. They looked like heat waves coming off hot pavement warmed by the sun—like flames emerging out of everything I saw. I was awestruck. It was only later that I realized what I had seen were the emanations of the Black Eagle described to Carlos Castaneda by his Toltec teacher, Don Juan.

Egyptians, on the other hand, identified the source of all reality as a black light associated with the Black Madonna, while Tibetans found the source of everything in a dark blue light similar to what we know today as ultraviolet light or the kind of black light often used in the entertainment industry to highlight fluorescent colors. Other spiritual traditions have taught that the manifest world emanates from a violet flame that is the source of Creation. Today, scientists speak of black holes and their role in creating the Universe. All of this seems to point to one all-powerful and vastly creative Source that brings light out of darkness. Shamans refer to this as Spirit. But it doesn't matter what we call it. And it doesn't matter how it appears to us. It is all the same, whether we refer to it as Oneness or God/Goddess or Spirit or Source.

Even though I spent a great deal of my later childhood in church praying, I didn't really believe that God was the source of my experience on a second-by-second basis. I thought of God as being somewhere higher in the sky—in heaven, a place removed from my reality. My God was separate from me and from my everyday experience, a God who mostly disapproved of my attempts to garner a little pleasure and avoid as much pain as I could. I believed that God thought of me as a lazy laggard who would probably never make it to heaven. This caused me to develop negative attitudes that, at the time, I thought were necessary. After all, I didn't want to commit the sin of pride and suffer an even worse fate.

Gradually, it dawned on me that if God is the Source of all Creation, then he must be inside and in between every particle of every electron of every atom in the Universe, including my own body. This came as a true revelation that motivated me to consider other "scandalous" and "heretical" thoughts as well. But even this realization didn't make it any easier for me to pay attention to Source. In no time, my thoughts drifted elsewhere and I found myself lost for days in the dream of everyday life without focusing my attention on Source at all. I was on the right track, but I didn't have all the answers to the questions that plagued me.

What did it mean that God was everywhere and inside of me as well? Did that mean that God and I were still separate beings? Could it possibly mean that God and I shared the same nature? Oh, blasphemy! Now I was on truly dangerous ground! Imagine the preposterous thought that there might not be that much difference between God's nature and my own. And if that were the case, could I really be such a lazy worm of a being? Did my even entertaining these thoughts insult God? Or could it be possible that an aspect of God actually *was* an incompetent laggard? So confusing!

Little by little, my understanding of this revelation grew, until I came to the inevitable conclusion that God *had* to be infinite. And if this were true, then I, by extension, was an expression of God. Slowly, the implications of the responsibility this entailed dawned on me. If I were truly an expression of God, then I had a duty to align myself with God's dream. I had to pay attention to my thoughts, feelings, and actions. I knew that I had been lazy, but instead of feeling shame and guilt over this, I was overcome with relief. How silly I had been!

Spirit, in fact, doesn't care if you realize you are part of God or not. But if you do realize it, God or Spirit is very happy because you are very happy. From the shamanic perspective, when you realize what Source is, you become more powerful and effective in the world. The more aware you are of Source, the more potent you become. All great shamans have a profound understanding of this fact, and this understanding makes them extremely powerful.

Later in my life, I found even greater inspiration in the words of the great teacher Eckhart Tolle, who tells us that God is like the sun, emanating rays of sunlight. These rays flow outward and through everything in the manifest world. Everything is bathed in the light of this sun and contains its rays. It's not that everything "is the sun"; it's rather that everything is "filled with the sun." And that makes sense to me. The divine flows through me and *is* me. I am not, however, the divine Source itself. But I can recognize the divine in others and all around me and in myself. And as I recognize it, I activate that which was already there and give it freedom through my choice to acknowledge it. I often find myself saying: "All is Divine, as am I." In fact, this is one of my most effective and powerful prayers. It is pure alchemy.

Spirit Is Everywhere

Although many believe that God is everywhere, we so easily forget this truth. And our forgetting is so complete that we engage in behaviors that are completely irrational—like war, murder, theft, lying, and mistreatment of others. This forgetting is also the source of dogmas that see God as a perfect being "up there," while we are wicked beings "down here." But how can God be "up there" if God is the Creator of everything from the inside out? Does this mean that God creates the evil of this world as well?

This is a hard question, but one from which we should not shrink. God creates sentient beings out of love and then gives them the free will to cocreate. People have the freedom to dream up events that are not loving, until they eventually remember who they are. God is responsible for everything that happens in the Universe, so God does allow foolish illusion to be created. But that does not mean that God gets pleasure out of the unloving acts that flow from this evil. To God, evil consists only of illusions that have no ultimate reality, because they are not in alignment with truth. This is very difficult to understand without a great deal of contemplation. To us, these painful events seem real in the here and now. But one day, we will realize that they are only a bad dream that vanishes in a sea of truth, love, and energy.

Sometimes it is very helpful to remind yourself *where* Spirit is. We so easily forget and become disconnected for a while. And it is this feeling of separation that leads to a sense of powerlessness. Spirit is not *elsewhere*; Spirit is *everywhere*. Spirit is *within* us. Prayer reminds us of where to find Spirit.

Partnering with Spirit

According to shamans and mystics the world over, there is great power in aligning with something greater than yourself. Don Guadalupe taught me that you always become more powerful when you associate with the greatest forces around you. So why not create a partnership with Spirit, the greatest force in the Universe? You have absolutely nothing to lose but misery and everything positive to gain. Offer your services to Spirit and see what happens. Of course, in all honesty, Spirit will probably test you to see if you are serious. But you must persevere in the face of challenging tests, no matter what.

Spirit is *big*—about as big as you can get. By contrast, we feel small. Yet there are those who manage to make their lives big despite that feeling. Gandhi was a man of small stature and slight build, but he shed a giant light on the world. The same is true for Nelson Mandela, Thich Nhat Hanh, Mother Teresa, the Dalai Lama, and many others. These great teachers have known that they are more than their relatively minor physical presence, because they are connected to the infinitely greater presence of Spirit. Thus they can play on a larger chessboard.

But there is an important difference between these great women and men and those who achieve great renown through tyranny. There is a difference between Gandhi and Hitler, for instance, or between Mandela and Osama bin Laden. The Gandhis of the world have real power because they have partnered with Spirit and Spirit works through them. Tyrants, on the other hand, merely play with the trappings of power to make up for their smallness and obvious limitations.

Ministers and priests often preach that we should be small and humble in the sight of God. They preach against vanity and warn of the sin of pride, threatening dire consequences from a wrathful God. This, of course, is nonsense. We are here to make a difference and that is hard to do when hiding our light under a bushel. When we partner with Spirit, we become expansive, influential, inspiring, and regal, even though we may still speak with a soft voice. Spirit is majestic and creates using a huge brush and a broad canvas. Spirit is within each of us and wants nothing more than to actualize, to self-realize, and to shine as bright a light as possible—like the sun. To shamans, each of us mirrors the sun, and the brighter we shine, the more of Spirit we manifest.

As human beings, we have the gift and the curse of free will; we can make endless choices. Sometimes our choices bring about great suffering; sometimes they bring about great joy. Sometimes we are unconscious of the choices we make; sometimes our choices are made by default. When we refuse to choose actively, however, we end up with less than happy results. But that is still a choice we make. There is no escaping free will. To become powerful, we must consciously choose the state of mind in which we wish to live.

We are always in the process of choosing, evolving, and realizing the full potential of the seed within us. We are always "becoming." Moreover, we choose what we will become. When we choose in partnership with Spirit, we accelerate our evolution immensely. It's not that there is any hurry in infinity, of course, but why not cut out some of the suffering? The following prayers can help you partner with Spirit to realize your full potential.

PRAYER FOR PARTNERSHIP

Great Spirit, you have made me

With the skill and knowledge of a master artist.

And you made me to create.

I Am a vessel for your inspiration.

Hands to build and shape;

My hands are your hands.

Eyes to witness;

My eyes are your eyes.

Ears to listen with compassion;

My ears are your ears.

A voice to sing and communicate;

My voice is your voice.

I Am your vehicle, your paintbrush.

I Am the story told *by* you and back *to* you, forever.

Great Spirit, *I Am* your partner and you are mine.

When you are with me, *I Am* whole.

When you are working with me, *I Am* healed.

Let us work together

To increase kindness and compassion,

To increase generosity and gratitude,

To fill the world with beauty, hope, and light.

And let us together join others in partnership in your name,

Until we have all remembered that we are one.

PRAYER TO CONNECT WITH SOURCE

Creator and Provider,

You are vast.

The farthest reaches of starry space cannot encompass you.

You supply every particle of the Universe.

You stretch in every direction to infinity.

You are all time, without limit.

You are the lightless light in the endless void.

You are the awesome sound of a great waterfall a thousand miles wide,

A trillion voices singing in harmony,

A billion drums beating in rhythm.

You are every instrument playing in the same instant,

A shattering symphony of energy and light.

And this great light, this magnificent song

Shines in me. Sings in me.

I Am vast.

I Am endless energy radiating.

My heart pours forth diamond light,

To engulf the Earth, the planets, and all space.

My mind expands to encompass your infinite light.

My mouth opens like a canyon to sing your truth.

I Am making a difference on this planet.

I Am participating in a massive awakening

With all my brothers and sisters.

Together we are powerful and we are great,

Because we are mirrored in your power.

Spirit of Space,

Spirit of Time,

Spirit of the Infinite.

PRAYER FOR CHOICE

Great Spirit,

I choose to awaken and remember.

I choose love.

I choose peace.

I choose to be generous.

I choose to celebrate.

I choose power, vitality, and health.

I choose to see your beauty in everything.

I choose prosperity and success.

I choose light and radiance.

I choose clarity and focus.

I choose to make the right choice.

I choose to align myself with your grand dream,

To persevere in knowing you,

To make you my guiding light.

Great Spirit, I choose your way,

Your path,

The path with heart.

Chapter 7

Prayers for Life's Challenges

You pray in your distress and in your need;
would that you might pray also in the fullness of
your joy and in your days of abundance.
—Kahlil Gibran, *The Prophet*

A number of years ago, my primary benefactor and shamanic teacher Guadalupe Candelario fell seriously ill, and we did not know what was wrong with him. At the time, by strange serendipity, he was working at an estate in Santa Fe, New Mexico, close to where Lena and I were living. We tried desperately to get him medical attention and finally got him admitted to a local hospital, where they discovered that he had a problem with his gallbladder. As they prepared him for surgery to remove it, we thought: "Oh good, they are going to solve the problem." We looked forward to him recovering quickly.

Little did we know that doctors had misdiagnosed him and that he was actually suffering from pancreatic cancer—probably as a result of having worked in the fields in Mexico where horrible pesticides were routinely used with no protection for those employed there for a pittance. The surgery was a disaster, and the cancer metastasized all through his bone marrow. He was sicker than ever and failing rapidly. The hospital discharged him, saying there was nothing more they could do. We were both distraught and furious with the medical establishment for their apparent helplessness. Guadalupe soon returned to his village in the Sierras to die.

This was one of the most emotionally painful experiences of my life. I was overwhelmed by helplessness, loss, anger, and abandonment. Lena and I drove 1,000 miles to see him one last time. Sick as he was, he was able to laugh and still teach us a thing or two. He told us not to worry and that he would always help us. And he has kept his word.

A few years later, Herlinda, one of our principal Shipibo teachers, fell ill, but stubbornly refused all help from Western medicine. She was eventually diagnosed with ovarian cancer, and although doctors recommended a complete hysterectomy, she refused. She was suspicious of allopathic medicine and began to fail.

My daughter, Anna, and I happened to be down in Peru leading a group of students. We went to see Herlinda in Lima, where she was staying temporarily with relatives. We found her gravely ill and dying. She instructed us in how to prepare her for death, because she had trained us for years and wanted us to help her cross over. Of course, we had no other choice but to step up to the task at hand because her relatives knew our abilities and preferred us to perform these tasks. It was extremely painful, but we did all we could for her. We followed all her instructions on how to use tobacco, *icaros*, and prayer to help her leave her body in a good way. Then we had to say goodbye, knowing that we would never see her again. Both of us learned a great deal in this process and again had to come to terms with one of life's great challenges.

The Challenge of Abandonment

Life is a never-ending cycle of change. All is impermanent, and everything created will be dissolved back into the void, whether we like it or not. This is one of the harder aspects of being human, because we become attached to many things—to our family and friends, to possessions and lifestyles, to our bodies and our looks, to pets, to working conditions, and so on. The only thing that is absolutely constant, however, is that everything is changing and will look very different in the future. The more we struggle to hang on to the status quo, the more painful the loss becomes when change occurs. We all need some help now and then letting go and detaching ourselves from the experiences and circumstances of our lives.

At the heart of loss is the experience of abandonment—one of the toughest challenges anyone can face. Everyone, no matter how blessed, has experienced moments of abandonment—perhaps when a friend or a pet dies, or when a relationship ends in divorce or breakup, when children leave home. Losing a job, moving, graduating, getting transferred, or going off to war are all experiences that can bring up feelings of abandonment. And these feelings can prompt a host of complex reactions and emotions like fear, desperation, anger, and ultimately grief.

Shamans use prayer to combat feelings of abandonment. When praying to address these feelings, they focus on the port on the top right side of the heart to which Essence connects (see chapter 3). They rely on their certainty that, no matter what happens, we are never, ever alone. We all have numerous internal guides and helping spirits who support us in every living moment of our lives.

Hard times are relative. I used to think that I had experienced some very hard times in my life. Like many others, I was beaten as a child; I was left behind for another; I was stolen from; I had serious accidents; I lost large sums of money; I was slandered and judged. Yet, compared to others, my difficulties have been minimal. I am extremely fortunate because I have had an extraordinary and wonderful life. When life gets hard, it may seem overwhelming and feel as if challenges will last forever. Fortunately, there are specific prayers to remedy hardship, and I will share them at the end of this chapter.

The Challenge of Separation

After working with thousands of people, including financially successful people, I have learned that life is very hard for almost everyone. This happens because we so easily fall into the trap of experiencing ourselves as separate and alone. This sense of isolation breeds deep fear—mostly fear of abandonment—something that is so painful it can actually lead to death.

At some point in our lives, we all experience the thoughtless actions of people who neglect our needs because they are caught up in their own dramas. Because we always do unto ourselves what was done unto us, we learn to abandon ourselves. And, because of a psychological defense mechanism called projection, this makes us feel that we have been abandoned by Spirit. In other words, we blame Spirit for what others and we ourselves have done. People seek therapy, take medication, and turn to many other remedies to heal from this terrible pain, In the end, however, there is really only one solution—to return to the source of the problem and reconnect to Spirit. This is not necessarily easy, but it is absolutely necessary for redemption and healing to occur. This is the shamanic way of healing.

Practicing a religion is often not the same thing as reconnecting to Spirit, however. While religion may help to a point, it can be precarious to place absolute faith in an organized system of beliefs, because dogma and external authority do not come from within. Religion often relies on a hope that something outside of ourselves will save us, and it so often disappoints. From the shamanic point of view, belief in an external power will never satisfy. The solution is "to know," and that comes from the heart alone.

You must know that Essence is within you at all times and that it is so powerful, so immense, so awesome that no name can ever adequately express it and no dogma can ever adequately explain it. The power of Essence is so expansive that most of us would be absolutely terrified if confronted with even a tiny fraction of it. And yet confront it we must, because it is the only reason we are alive; without it, we would all vanish instantly. Every great spiritual tradition teaches this unequivocally. And yet we don't listen, and we persist in becoming horribly lost.

I experienced one manifestation of the difference between religion and Spirit in the practice of confession. As a young Catholic boy, I was taught to confess my sins to the parish priest in a little closet at the side of the church. I was terrified of confession because I never felt comfortable confessing to a priest I didn't even know, especially when he wanted to know all the most private details of my life. I felt shamed, and even more ashamed when I reported the same set of sins week after week. This man was supposed to represent God, but I can see in retrospect that he was just as human as I was. As I got older, I rejected the practice of confession, considering it to be barbaric and unaligned with my view of Spirit.

Surprisingly, I learned the value of confession from the Huichol people. Although not originally Catholic, they regularly and publicly confess their sins to Tatewari—"grandfather fire"—during all-night ceremonies. They tie a knot in a string for each *pecado*—those things they feel are out of harmony or imbalanced within their own integrity. When the knots are tied, they throw the string into the fire and watch it burn, while asking forgiveness of all their neighbors who are watching as witnesses. At the end of the ceremony, the entire village is harmonized and healed. Tears are shed; hugs are shared; and relationships are renewed. Hard feelings are released and forgiveness is given. Similar ceremonies are performed in some Buddhist traditions.

From a shamanic perspective, you don't need an intermediary to confess your sins. Confession is merely a process through which you release and forgive yourself. So confessing to "the fire," or to a mirror, or to a journal, or to a loved one are all wonderfully effective. And this is the shaman's way.

The Challenge of Anxiety

When I was younger, I spent too much of my valuable time feeling anxious and worried. I can honestly say that it never helped me at all. While intellectually most of us can see that worry and anxiety are a terrible waste of time, it can be difficult to let these feelings go because they are such a pervasive and fundamental part of our experience as human beings. We are mortal creatures who seem to be trapped in bodies that can be hurt, maimed, or killed. We have sensitive emotional systems that can be attacked and undermined. We are sentient creatures who are capable of thinking abstractly and thus projecting into the future. And all of these characteristics contribute to feelings of anxiety and fear.

Our ability to project into the future and remember the past is both a blessing and a curse. The blessing derives from our ability to create goals, plan for the new circumstances, learn from our mistakes, and compile knowledge. The curse lies in the fact that we remember pain and horror from the past and worry about it occurring again in the future. We can project all manner of fears into the future, and doing so raises our stress level enormously. Tell a horse that it will be put to sleep at dawn and it will make no difference to the horse at all. Tell a person that there is a possibility he or she will be executed at dawn and that person will most likely fall prey to fear and anxiety, even if execution is only a remote possibility.

When dealing with anxiety, you have to commit yourself to easing it. You must learn not to indulge in fear, because fear just begets more fear and more fear and more fear. From personal experience, I know that reducing anxiety must become a discipline. If you can't discipline yourself to overcome your fears, all the outside help in the world will not do it for you.

For shamans, anxiety is just a huge energy leak that robs you of the possibility of breaking free. To become powerful, you must erase it at its source. The good news is that prayer is an effective way to deal with worry and anxiety, and I have included prayer to help with that at the end of this chapter.

The Challenge of Anger

One manifestation of fear is anger. And this bears repeating. *The foundation of anger is always fear.* This is important to know because, until we realize this, there is no escape from the anger trap. Most of the time, our anger just wastes energy and is unproductive, although there are times when righteous anger can actually help motivate us to accomplish great things and survive otherwise fatal experiences. Unfortunately, this type of anger is far less common, and discriminating between using anger as a tool for change and letting it drain our energy resources takes great wisdom. And on the way to that wisdom, we make many mistakes.

For most of us, managing anger is one of life's greatest challenges, and the Information Age is making that even more difficult. Turn on any television or computer and it won't be long before you see injustice toward the planet, cruelty to animals, or mistreatment of people.

We're often given mixed signals about how to deal with our anger, and we might be tempted to completely ignore or suppress these feelings, but the only way to escape from the negative effects of anger is to admit being angry. When we deny that we are angry, it only makes our anger worse and builds up resentment that acts like a slow poison, killing off aliveness. Being truthful about being angry is, in fact, the first step to escaping it. But there is a big difference between expressing anger and admitting it. Expressing anger or acting it out is usually destructive and expands our pain. Admitting anger, on the other hand, is constructive because it recognizes what we are feeling and removes our resistance to it. Later in this chapter, I give an example of a prayer to confront and neutralize anger.

The Challenge of Habits

Prayer can also help us to overcome destructive habits. On one hand, habits help us learn. We learn to type by teaching our fingers to go to certain keys out of habit. We learn to speak a language by habitually speaking specific sounds in a certain order. Likewise, habits help us learn to drive a car or operate machinery. But habits can become destructive when we go beyond them or let them take over so we cannot move on to other things. Habits are part of our survival machinery, but when they get out of control, they can also harm us or even kill us.

Industrial psychology uses the phrase "transfer of error" to describe behaviors that can lead to fatal mistakes. Back in the sixties, engineers modified a switch used to turn on the auxiliary gas tank in a certain model of small plane by changing the direction in which it moved. The results were catastrophic. Pilots who were running out of gas in the main tank and had to turn on the auxiliary gas tank rapidly in order to avoid crashing had to fumble with an unfamiliar control. This resulted in many crashes—and many lawsuits.

My shaman teachers explained this from a different perspective. Habits, they believe, can make us too predictable and that makes us vulnerable. Because a prairie dog predictably rises out of its hole when the air reaches 68 degrees, all a hawk has to do is wait until the air reaches that temperature and it can have lunch. The extent to which we are utterly predictable is the extent to which we can be manipulated. That's why advertising works so well.

Sometimes we form habits that can be quite harmful. And when these habits get a grip on us, they become addictions. When a habit becomes an addiction, we lose control over ourselves, and that is dangerous. An addiction usually involves one of the pleasure centers of the body that gives a feeling of temporary relief from the pain we feel inside. The more serious addictions, like alcohol and drugs, can lead to self-destruction.

The ancient mystery schools taught that the color violet is a powerful healer of addictions. You can work with this color when you feel threatened by an addiction. Imagine immersing yourself for a few minutes in a violet light. Try running a violet-colored flame through your thoughts to clear them out. Lavender can also be used as an effective tool to fight addiction. Rubbing lavender oil on your hands or breathing its fragrance can help to relieve of the stress that leads to addictions and the pressure that comes from them. Shamans of the Amazon use this method to help combat addiction to cocaine and other scourges for which people seek cures.

To be clear, while prayer may not cure a severe habit or addiction all by itself, it can certainly support you in your struggle to overcome them. I give you an example below.

Prayers to Overcome Challenges

Here I will give you examples of prayers that you can use to overcome some of the challenges we have discussed. As always, you can use them as they stand or adapt them to fit your needs. You can also let them inspire you to create your own personal prayers.

PRAYER TO HEAL DEPRESSION

Great Spirit,

Even through these difficult hours

I know you are supporting me.

You are my Source

And I know you are with me and love me.

Even when I flounder and forget how to

Keep my head above the dark waters,

I know your light is shining within me.

You overflow with abundant gifts.

You created me and *I Am* grateful for my life.

When the wind rises and I falter, out of control,

You are there to set the sail and show me the way home.

And in the smallest, deepest hours of night,

When I feel the most alone and my mind plays tricks—

Trying to make me believe *I Am* disconnected, lost, without hope—

Spirit, I know in the heart of my heart that you are always here

With me, all around me, inside me.

You are here with me in this very moment,

Creating me in this very moment.

You made me for the sole purpose of knowing you,

Creating with you.

You are infinitely powerful

And everything that you are, *I Am* also.

I Am healed and whole.

I Am connected.

I Am deeply loved.

I Am filled with your light.

I Am truth, love, and power.

Thank you for these gifts.

PRAYER TO REDUCE ANXIETY

Notice that, in the prayer below, anxiety is expressed in the past, while calm is expressed in the present. Even if you are very anxious, saying this prayer will begin to calm you. Ancient shamans used a technique to enhance its effect. You can calm yourself by cleaning your hands and rubbing the roof of your mouth with your thumb for a few minutes before and after you say this prayer. This is what small children naturally do to calm themselves as they fall asleep.

Great Provider,

I have sometimes worried myself sick,

Traveling far into the future and being caught in a
web of what-ifs.

And in times like these, my heart has hammered
in my chest,

And I have felt utterly alone—adrift on a cold dark sea.

Yet, even in these times, though I may have forgotten,

You are still here with me—in the very center
of my being.

In these moments, Spirit, help me to remember

I Am at home in my heart.

I Am breathing, in and out.

I Am still; *I Am* calm; *I Am* at peace.

Help me to remember that all I have to do is
ask for your help.

And with your help, *I Am* relaxed.

With your help, *I Am* present in this moment.

I know my visions of the future have not been real.

This moment is real.

The what-ifs, the maybes, have not been real.

I Am real, and *I Am* right here right now.

What will be will simply be.

I Am here with a purpose.

I Am endlessly supported.

And I have a contribution to make.

My job is to do my best and not to worry.

I Am calm now.

I Am calm now.

I Am calm now.

PRAYER TO MANAGE LOSS

Great Spirit,

You have given me my life.

You have given me all the people that I love—

Pets to love,

Places to live and work,

Things I have grown accustomed to.

All this, you gave to me,

And I wanted them to stay here with me forever.

I wanted to believe nothing would change.

But when that illusion shattered, I became angry.

I became angry with you for taking them away,

Leaving me alone, frightened, and heartbroken.

And then I remembered that

You never promised forever—not to me, or to anyone.

These are temporary gifts, precious and rare.

I Am grateful for the blessing of their presence

And I know, too, that they are not truly gone,

That all forms change

And that you are in all things and beings.

They have transformed into something new,

Like new spring flowers born from old wintered earth.

It's natural and good to cry—to mourn this loss,

To release this grief.

But I also release them out into a new adventure,

One that I will take someday myself.

And in that way we have never parted.

I accept this is the way of things.

I know that you are with me even in my grief.

This is the way it has always been.

This is the way it should be.

Spirit, with your help, I can let go

And find peace.

PRAYER TO QUELL ANGER

Creator,

I have felt the burning heat of anger rising in me,

Seizing the reins of my thoughts, my words, my self-control.

I have wanted to take revenge,

To make someone pay,

To protect my ego.

I have been angry because I was hurt,

Because I was disappointed,

Because I was afraid,

Because I was embarrassed.

I imagined myself to be in charge,

To be the judge of right and wrong.

But only you can truly know the whole picture.

Spirit, I ask you to show me what I need to learn.

My anger has kept me from knowing you better.

Help me forgive myself for getting angry,

To let go of this burden and move on.

Help me to find the best way to speak truth to injustice,

And to always seek compassion and forgiveness.

That is what I intend.

That is what I want.

That is what is best.

I Am at peace.

PRAYER TO COMBAT ADDICTIONS

Imagine a violet light flowing through your body as you pray the following prayer.

Great Provider,

I have been in the grip of something fierce.

I thought I could manage it, but I have been out of control.

It has felt as though a demon had taken over my life.

It promised me the world, but I became a slave to it.

It has felt like it could kill me if I let it.

But *I will not* let it.

I know that I was meant for better things,

That you created me to be healthy and whole,

To be your instrument of inspiration and kindness.

Spirit, please help me to change my direction.

Give me the strength to banish this demon from my life.

I know you will not abandon me

And I know that every time I fall I will get up again.

With each passing day, I will become even more dedicated

To living free and independently.

I will be victorious,

First in heart, then in mind, then in body.

And through you, I will find that, each day,

I love myself more,

I honor myself more.

I will look this demon in the eye and say,

"I no longer yield one second of power to you!

You are no longer part of my life or my world!

You have no power over me!"

I receive love.

I have purpose and meaning.

I honor and respect myself.

I Am victorious.

Chapter 8

Prayers for Health and Healing

*Prayer is the key of the morning
and the bolt of the evening.*
—Mahatma Gandhi

From a shamanic point of view, our bodies are based on a blueprint, a perfect energetic design that produces a perfectly functioning being with optimal health. This perfect pattern even lies beneath the physical and mental challenges of people born with disabilities. Through accident, illness, age, and trauma, our bodies fall into disrepair. But great saints and shamans have demonstrated again and again that they can restore bodies to their original perfection with a touch, a sound, a breath. Jesus made the blind see, the deaf hear, and the lame walk. But he is by no means the only one with this power.

Tibetan Buddhists hiss very quietly to alter aspects of the 72,000 nadis that make up the subtle nervous system of our physical and energetic bodies, returning them to their primary perfection. Shipibo shamans heal by singing repairs into the energetic tapestry of the body based on this perfect design. The Diné (Navajo) of the American Southwest, Chinese Taoists, and most shamans I have met in other traditions understand the importance of speaking directly to any diseased organs to return them to health and integrate them with the rest of the body. When particular organs become isolated, unhappy, or cut off, they can malfunction or become diseased. Talking to them acknowledges them, gives them positive attention, and makes them feel loved. They are more likely to heal when they are addressed directly and with love.

The Inner Smile

Knowing that your health is founded in a perfect architectural design is very useful, because it gives you an original state of perfection to which you can return. When our bodies do not work right, when events go wrong in our world, we may turn against whatever body part is troubling us. Yet rejecting or dismissing what hurts only makes our ailments worse. We only heal when our thoughts are positive and our attitude joyful. In a sense, we only heal when we smile.

Taoist shamans in ancient China knew that the act of smiling could produce profoundly positive physiological effects—both on the body and on other objects. They used this knowledge to create a powerful contemplation they called "the inner smile." They believed that the Tao—All that Is—exists in a perpetual state of happiness and reasoned that, when we smile along with the Tao, we align ourselves with the most powerful healing force in the Universe.

Likewise, the Toltecs teach of a cosmic smile that may visit us in our dreams while "dreaming awake," as they say. This smile may appear as simple crescent moons, or smiling mouths, or whole smiling faces. Indeed, for them, the most profound smiles are the gummy grins of old crones with missing teeth. These smiles indicate that we are on the right shamanic path—the path of healing and knowing.

Today, Western researchers corroborate what the Taoists and the Toltecs discovered long ago and validate their beliefs. Smiling and laughing *do* produce a great variety of positive effects on the body. This does not mean that producing a fake smile to mask your real feelings is an effective strategy, however. The inner smile of the Taoists and the cosmic smile of the Toltecs are effective because they are grounded in a critical "inner state," not just in a false external facial expression.

In order to practice the inner smile, sit, stand, lie, or walk quietly and peacefully. Close your eyes two-thirds of the way and produce an ineffable smile on your face, like that of the *Mona Lisa*—not a great big grin, just a slight smile. Then direct your attention toward whatever is troubling you and, without expanding your external smile, produce a great big internal smile. If you have been suffering from a stomachache or a pain in your back, direct your smile toward these areas. If you have been having difficulty with a person or a situation at work, direct your smile at them. Maintain each focus for a least several minutes.

If you have difficulty smiling because you are simply in a rotten mood, begin by focusing on something that always tends to make you smile—your dog, your kitten, your granddaughter, or your favorite nephew. And you can always encourage your inner smile with a prayer. I will give you an example later in the chapter.

The Immune System

Our modern way of life poses great challenges for our immune systems. Toxins, pesticides, food additives, chemical compounds, vaccines, and medications can all play havoc with our bodies' protection system. The thymus gland, located below the thyroid gland under the throat, is central to our immune system. In infants, this gland is disproportionally large and takes up most of the upper chest, but by the time we are adults, it has shrunk down to a more proportional size. The thymus is constantly stressed and overwhelmed by negative physiological and environmental influences and often exhausts itself by the time we reach middle age.

There is an exercise you can do to support your thymus and increase the effectiveness of your immune system. Sit quietly and locate your thymus gland by placing the fingers of either hand in the V cleft in your throat and moving down a couple of inches. Gently rest your fingers on that spot. Don't apply pressure, just let your thymus gland become aware of the helping fingers that are beckoning it just outside the skin. Focus on the thought that your thymus gland is so glad you are attending to it that it readily reaches out for your fingers. Envision your fingers gently beckoning and ever-so-slightly pulling on your thymus, but don't actually do anything.

Now focus on the *I Am* point in your heart—the port through which you connect to Essence—and feel yourself being there, creating a loving connection to your thymus gland. When it experiences this love, it will automatically begin to heal itself in whatever way is necessary. You can do this for any organ in your body. This process doesn't take long—usually under a minute and possibly only a few seconds. If you wish, you can pray while holding your fingers in position. (I will give you an example below.) When you are ready, lower your hand and be sure to drink plenty of fluids to support this cleansing.

Exhaustion

Western science has now proven that sleep is essential for optimal health. Shamans have known this for centuries and go even further, saying that exhaustion is an unnatural condition of being cut off from the great source of vitality and power within Essence. The short-term solution for exhaustion is, of course, rest. The long-term solution is to restore your connection to Essence and thus to Spirit.

In this stressful world, we sometimes have difficulty sleeping. About half of all Americans have trouble sleeping at least twice a week, and some have trouble all the time. Doctors prescribe sleeping pills, but they stop working after a time and interrupt the deep regeneration that real sleep provides. They may work in a pinch, but they are not a good solution in the long run.

The reason why we can't get to sleep or why we wake up in the middle of the night is either that we are disturbed by emotions that bring us back to physical waking or our energetic balance has been disturbed by bad habits. These emotions and imbalances interrupt our sleep cycle, influence our thoughts, and distort our sense of reality. We suffer from these conditions because we feel cut off from our deepest Source, Spirit. When these emotions and imbalances persist, even a full eight hours of sleep don't help and we wake up more exhausted than when we went to bed. When we are truly connected to Source, however, we get the sleep and the rest we need, even though our sleep cycle may be brief.

According to the Toltecs, we fail to gain the advantages that dreaming offers because we don't remember our dreams or don't understand their importance or the symbols that appear in them. To make their dreams much more effective, they practice lucid dreaming and actively work with the symbols that appear in their dreams to change the narrative of their lives. While most people believe that dreamless sleep makes for a good night's rest, the Toltecs believe just the opposite. They believe that a night of dreaming helps rejuvenate the body and has many other positive consequences for their lives. Paradoxically, the Toltec dream masters don't have what other people call ordinary dreams; they experience real events during hypnogogic trances. They actively cultivate dreaming while awake through shamanic practices and by taking herbs that stimulate the dreaming process. By combining this with special prayers, they achieve what they call "flowering" (self-realization) and change the narrative of their lives for the better. I will give you a sample prayer below.

Sex

People are seldom neutral about sex. They are either starving for it, or feel guilty over it, or experience shame about it, or hate it, or want to indulge in it with someone new, or are too exhausted for it. They are bored by it, stressed about it, try to ignore or resist it, or indulge in it excessively. Very few people claim to have a perfect sex life and, if they do have, it general succombs to illness, travel, work, death, or stress. Sex is just not a neutral thing. It is tied up with self-esteem, health, self-image, partnership, temporary feelings, and a host of other influences. The bottom line is that most people wish they had a better relationship with sex, just as they wish they had a better relationship with their bodies.

Many people don't feel comfortable praying about sex, because they feel ashamed to think about it while talking to God. But this is absurd. Spirit created sex, and it is an important part of healthy life. Of course God knows all about sex, and of course it is perfectly acceptable to talk to Spirit about sex. After all, Spirit is constantly combining and recombining to become One.

Shamans across many cultures consider sexual energy to be the foundation of personal power. They discipline themselves to build up this store of energy so they can transmute it for healing and awakening to wisdom. For them, sexual energy is a sacred trust that is not to be squandered or tainted by either excess or shame. Sexual energy is what powers their dreaming and their magical flights to discover the knowledge and tools of transformation. Below, I include a prayer that you can use to acknowledge and sanctify your sexuality.

Healing Prayers

Here I give you examples of prayers that you can use to manage the conditions and ailments we have discussed. As always, you can use them as they stand or adapt them for your own purposes. You can also be inspired by them to create your own personal prayers.

PRAYER FOR SMILING

This prayer can facilitate your smiling contemplation of health. Feel free to adapt it by adding as many other parts of your body as you wish. Or you can combine parts of your body to move quickly through the prayer. This exercise can be used as a healthy refreshing start to the day or to heal a particular part of your body that is troubling you.

Great Spirit,

I Am alive and this fills me with joy

That radiates out through my smile.

I smile with you and to you, Spirit,

And I thank you for my life.

Now I smile at you, feet;

You support me so well.

I smile at you, knees;

You are most flexible and durable.

I smile at you, belly;

Reservoir of power that you are.

I smile at you, lungs;

You breathe life into me and fill me with power.

I smile at you, heart;

Great volumes of life-giving blood flow through me.

I smile at you, spine;

You carry critically important messages to my body.

I smile at you, arms;

You are so good at holding and reaching.

I smile at you, eyes;

Seeing is such delight.

I smile at you, ears;

Such music you allow me to hear.

I smile at you, brain;

For, with you, I'm sane.

And I smile at all the rest—

This whole miraculous temple

That holds and contains Spirit,

This small part of a vast Creation.

PRAYER FOR PERFECT HEALTH

Great Spirit, you have given me a magical body

And I know that there have been times when

I didn't know how to best take care of it.

But now I know that my body wants to heal,

That it is always restoring itself,

That *I Am* healing right now, in this very moment.

I Am returning to perfection.

Every cell in my body is remembering its original design.

Every part of my body is bursting with vitality,
youth, and vigor.

Every organ of my body is remembering its perfect
structure.

My skin is restoring itself to perfect health.

My brain is remembering how to rest in health
and peace.

My chest, lungs, and heart are all returning to
perfection.

All the marvelous parts of my being are becoming
young again,

Working perfectly, optimally, full of strength and energy.

I Am recovering the perfect, beautiful blueprint of
my body.

I Am whole.

I Am restored.

I Am healed.

PRAYER FOR SLEEP

This prayer can slow the mind and help you let go of
the day. It may be helpful to repeat it several times as
you fall asleep.

Spirit, the day has ended and the sun has set,

And *I Am* ready to rest, cradled in your heart within
my heart.

I Am letting go of the day, my waking dream,

To enter into the deeper dream.

Restore me, revitalize me, heal me during my rest.

Allow this breath to carry me to your depths.

With each breath, my mind releases;

My body relaxes into peace and tranquility,

Deeper and deeper into the vast and timeless reaches

Of peace,

Of rest,

Of sleep.

PRAYER FOR RENEWAL

Spirit, tomorrow is a new day,

Full of the potential for vitality, power, and purpose.

I know every particle of my being will receive refreshment as I sleep.

Every cell is healing and returning to its original perfect state.

Every limitation is releasing.

All obstacles are removed.

Every doubt is banished.

All sorrow is cleansed.

I will awake renewed, radiating goodness.

When the sun dawns on a new day, Spirit,

Help me to wake with a new clarity of vision

And a clear path through every challenge.

Flood me with blessings so that, when I awaken,

I Am prepared to serve you, others, and myself.

PRAYER FOR COPING WITH ILLNESS

Spirit,

The doctors say I have a serious illness,

That there is something wrong in my body.

I have many choices facing me,

And I have felt overwhelmed and frightened and lost.

And I have been angry and confused.

And I have had moments of dark despair.

But Great Spirit, I know

That whatever the choices and whatever the outcome,

I still have you.

You are my awareness, my aliveness, my Source,

The source of my warmth and vitality.

I Am alive in this moment.

I Am conscious in this moment.

I Am connected with you in *every* moment.

You are here deep in my heart.

So I choose to focus on you, my Source, with every second I have,

To feel you radiating out from my heart

And flooding my body with light—

Light that consumes all doubt and distortion,

Leaving only strength and peace.

This powerful golden light floods outward

To every cell, in every breath.

There is no limit to the golden light.

You are here, *I Am* here.

I Am strong.

I Am whole.

I Am at peace.

PRAYER FOR REVITALIZATION

This prayer can restore connection with Spirit so that you once again feel revitalized and rested.

Creator,

I have been very tired, out of energy.

Yet, though I have felt exhausted,

Within my heart you are vital as ever.

And with your help,

I Am taking care of myself now.

I Am resting deeply.

I Am reestablishing my connection with you.

I feel your strength and aliveness

Spreading slowly outward like a warm glow of light.

I feel your love for me pouring forth,

Radiating out throughout my body,

Restoring, refreshing, revitalizing.

In your light

I Am healed.

I Am strong.

I Am renewed.

PRAYER FOR BALANCED SEXUALITY

Spirit, thank you for giving me a body,

Capable of pleasure.

My sexuality has its tides, its peaks and valleys.

Thank you for helping me to understand this.

Thank you for helping me to know that desire is natural.

Let me share this with the right person.

Let us delight in each other's bodies.

And let this sharing always be with one who is my equal,

With one who consents and has the maturity to know what they want.

Let this person delight in me, and I in them.

I Am a sexual being.

I Am a beautiful sexual being.

May I express my sexuality completely naturally

As does everything in nature.

Chapter 9

Prayers for Cultivating Virtues

*It is better in prayer to have a heart
without words than words without a heart.*

—John Bunyan

Rafael, one of our Huichol teachers and a praying powerhouse, shared a story with me during an all-night peyote ceremony. When he was a child, his family was so poor that they frequently had nothing to eat. They lived hand to mouth, and sometimes he was very cold because he had no jacket to protect him from the cold winters of the Sierras where they lived. As he recalled those difficult times, his eyes filled with tears. "But," he said, "Spirit always provided and somehow, some way, we survived and eventually thrived." He showed no sign of feeling sorry for himself. Rather he was simply speaking the truth and making the point that, for him, Spirit was all important. By honoring Spirit and giving thanks for what they did have, he made it through.

From a shamanic perspective, one of our greatest obstacles is the tendency to feel sorry for ourselves over what happens in life. When we feel like victims, we blame others and see them as predators and oppressors. By doing so, we empower them with our own fears. This undermines us and energizes the most primitive instincts of others. No one wins. It takes discipline to erase these thoughts of victimization and feelings of martyrdom. We can't afford to allow our thoughts to stray there even briefly. But there is a tried-and-true method for releasing our feelings of martyrdom—one that is ancient and has been taught in many mystery schools throughout the ages.

The antidote for martyrdom is to see yourself as a *cause* rather than an *effect*. This doesn't mean seeing yourself as deserving of blame, however. It simply means that you take responsibility for what you experience. Remember, the word *responsible* means "response able"; it means that you are able to respond.

Here, I am not implying that your everyday personality or ego can overcome your feelings of victimization. Rather, I mean to say that your deeper, more expansive self—Essence—can help you overcome them. By reinforcing your identification with Essence and relaxing your identification with your ego or false self, you can rise above these feelings. Remember, your ego is just a pawn in life. If you identify with it, you find yourself in deep trouble.

Rejecting Martyrdom

On this planet, with its almost eight billion people, it is easy to feel small and overlooked. This makes us insecure, and we try to put on a self-important facade in hopes that we will stand out from the crowd and be given special attention and honor. Put simply, we just want to feel special, loved, and nurtured. In shamanic terms, this tendency toward self-importance becomes a massive obstacle to our freedom, because, as long as we are enslaved by this need, we are limited and constrained. Shamans teach that self-importance must be banished, no matter how hard the task. Sometimes shamans and spiritual teachers use fairly brutal methods to rid their apprentices of this scourge. Fortunately, Don Guadalupe and my other teachers did not employ these methods, but taught that compassion and subtlety were the best practices to turn me away from my own self-importance.

Jealousy, misunderstanding, envy, competition, and fear will always be a part of our world. No matter how nice you are, it is inevitable that, at some time and in some place, you will interact with people who don't have your best interests at heart. Shamans are acutely aware of this and have developed numerous techniques for dealing with it. For them, releasing yourself from feelings of martyrdom and victimization are a matter of life and death. People who victimize and oppress you can make your life miserable, but they can also teach you many valuable lessons about yourself. I have had my share of these people in my life—one took a woman I loved away from me; one ruined a book project; another stole vast sums of money from me; and yet another succeeded in eliminating a teaching job I truly loved because she was envious of my high student evaluations and disagreed with my philosophy. But these experiences have taught me more than I could ever have imagined. They showed me where my fears limited me, where my insecurities thwarted my desires, and where I needed clearer boundaries.

Many people unfortunately have been conditioned to wear their suffering like a badge of honor. They feel it entitles them to retribution and revenge. Life does come with inevitable pain, but long suffering is more of a choice. Suffering, like fear, begets more of itself, and shamanically speaking becomes a huge energy leak. Pain can teach us, but suffering has no such saving graces. Martyrs tend to want others to join them in their misery and secretly seek to punish others for their unhappiness. Their complaining is intended to make others feel guilty, but in reality it tends to irritate other people to exasperation. They do not realize that behind their martyrdom is the universal desire to be loved.

At the deepest levels of our being, we all want to be connected, loved, and nurtured. On a spiritual level, this is easier for us to comprehend. On a physical level, however, this sometimes feels like a lie. Many of us spend a lifetime looking for that one special person who is our soul mate, the one who will make everything feel right and complete. But we seldom find that fantasy person; instead, we find ourselves surrounded by real live people who are sometimes flawed, defensive, insecure, and fearful. We are afraid of these people because they are too much like us. And since we don't accept ourselves, we don't want to accept them. We avoid getting close to them because we are afraid that we may want more than they can give. We fear that they may become too dependent or that they may reflect our own vulnerabilities and flaws. And we fear we may be abandoned by these very people we judge to be flawed themselves. What a dilemma!

The only solution is to love everyone who is here on Earth with us. We have to let down our guard, take a risk, and allow ourselves to be vulnerable, while at the same time exercising good judgment. But how can we evaluate and judge others and at the same time remain available to them? That is not as difficult as it may seem. It is our job to be available. Spirit never judges, so why should we? We can be discerning instead.

Embracing Wisdom

During the years of my apprenticeship with Guadalupe, he returned over and over to the theme of integrity and living a life that reflects wisdom. He said that living a life without integrity—colored by dishonesty and poor judgment—was like letting a band of thieves into your house and watching them strip it bare. He said that, once you begin on the shamanic path and acknowledge this, it will go much harder on you if you choose to lose your integrity than it would have if you had never started on that path. His repetition of this theme and the seriousness with which he expressed it made a deep impression on me. I listened.

And now I repeat his wisdom to others, because it has always proven to be true. As I look around at the world, I see the consequences all around me for those who do not maintain their integrity. I want to tell them: No! Stop! You are headed for the cliff! But I don't. Because this is the way that most of us learn—the hard way. We make our choices and experience the consequences. After all, Spirit gave us the freedom to make mistakes.

But information is not wisdom; simply having knowledge about something doesn't mean that you understand it. You can have knowledge of a minefield, but unwisely walk there anyway. Wisdom is something that is not limited to the workings of the brain. You can be exceptionally smart and yet not be wise, as many a criminal can attest. So, what is wisdom? Wisdom is rather something that you accumulate over a long, gradual life-education. It is the ability to see the big picture and understand what you are looking at in the context of what is best for the greatest good. Wisdom implies developed values, perceiving in a way that others may not have been able to achieve. That is why we seek out shamans and wise teachers to help us.

A person with wisdom always keeps an open heart, because that is where wisdom resides. Yet being wise does not mean being emotional or sentimental. A wise person is kind, but not overly protective; understanding, but not fawning; loving, but capable of being ruthlessly truthful. A wise person does not blink or avoid your eyes when listening to you. A wise person does more listening than speaking. Wisdom may be spoken by the young, and it may be lost on the elderly. Most of all, a wise person has a deep connection to Spirit and understands how insignificant we are in the larger scheme of things. I include a prayer for wisdom at the end of this chapter.

Unconditional Love

There is no more important human experience than to love and be loved. Although affection comes naturally to us, as it does to all mammals, we must cultivate the ability to truly love, and this only happens over a long period of time. Too often, our primitive attempts to love are actually conditional. "If you give me things, I will love you." "If you do as I say, I will love you." "If you are nice to me, I will love you." Eventually, however, after many difficult lessons, we learn to love unconditionally. But this takes a lot of experience and grappling with the consequences of our failures.

Another challenge is to learn to love *ourselves* unconditionally. This is even harder, because to do so, we must get past all our self-loathing, self-deprecation, low self-esteem, and an inability to forgive ourselves for not being perfect. One important aspect of loving yourself is knowing that you are loved and allowing that love to penetrate from the outside in—or to emerge from the inside out. There is a kind of chicken-or-the-egg quality to all this. What comes first, learning to love yourself or learning to love others? Learning to let love in or learning to project the love you feel for yourself?

The only way we can truly learn to love is first to be loved, because this is a necessary requirement for unconditional love to flourish. People and animals who have been shown no love are often mean, cruel, ruthless, angry, or unresponsive. But even when we aren't shown love at a young age, it is still possible for us to become loving ourselves. In order for this to happen, however, we must recognize, at the deepest levels, that love is the substance of Creation and therefore fuels every particle of the Universe.

If this is true, however, how can it be that at times we feel unloved? Sometimes we are so close to the truth that we fail to see it. Like the proverbial nose on our faces, we are so busy looking past it that we cannot find it. We are in a state of ignorance or illusion when we believe that love is something we find outside ourselves. It can certainly feel that way when our bodies seek visible and tangible signs of affection. But love is ultimately found at the very core of our awareness. To discover it, we have to learn to look within. This is not something that we are taught to do, nor is it something that we find gratifying at first.

Shamanically speaking, the spiritual colors of love are rose-pink and ruby. This is why people give pink or red roses to express their love. If you choose to, you can encourage love by flooding yourself, especially your heart, with these colors while you pray. This can help to make your prayer much more powerful. I give you a shamanic prayer to cultivate love at the end of this chapter.

Forgiveness

The act of forgiveness is closely related to love. Nonetheless, as we all know, forgiving those who hurt us is a profound challenge. We are afraid at the deepest levels that, if we forgive those who have offended us in some way, this will let them off the hook and they won't have to pay for what they did. Or even worse, we may feel that they will hurt us all over again. We worry that, if we forgive others, we will make ourselves vulnerable, so we withhold that forgiveness in order to remain vigilant.

Carrying blame and resentment against others is a poison that none of us can afford in our lives. The person who is most hurt by my lack of forgiveness is myself. We must gradually learn to forgive, simply because we are made in the image of the Creator and the Creator forgives all. But there is a difference between forgiving others and naively excusing bad behavior. We have to learn to forgive others while still setting boundaries and taking care of ourselves.

For instance: "I forgive you your debt, but never ask me for money again."

Moreover, forgiving ourselves for mistakes we have made can be even harder than forgiving others. Most of us are very hard on ourselves, and we need help allowing forgiveness in. We hold ourselves hostage to our mistakes, but this is horrifically destructive and usually results in us punishing ourselves with cancers, accidents, business losses, and failed relationships. We must learn to forgive ourselves even if what we have done has itself been extremely harsh and destructive. When we are afraid that, if we let ourselves off the hook, we will just repeat the same offense, we withhold the forgiveness that could keep us on the straight path.

From a shamanic point of view, failing to forgive keeps us from being better human beings. It keeps us stuck in behaviors that make us deeply miserable and results in a horrible loss of power. Think of it as being constipated, with nothing flowing and everything stopped up. When we no longer flow, we become unhealthy, and that is limiting for Essence expression.

Besides, who are we not to forgive ourselves when the Creator forgives all immediately? Spirit is invested in us moving on, because it knows that is the road to happiness and eventual fulfillment. Spirit wants to experience fulfillment through each of us.

It wants all of us to come home to celebrate reunion with the infinite. The natural balance of life is to forgive, a process that completes and closes the circle.

To forgive means to give something back. When we forgive, we give freedom back to others and to ourselves. We give space to create our lives fresh and new. We give expansion and love. That is why forgiveness is considered divine. It is! While asking for forgiveness is healing, it is even more healing to forgive yourself as a way to reassert your connection to Spirit. Spirit doesn't really care if you miss the mark. It knows humans are going to miss the mark, because the Creator made humankind to evolve through learning—and this involves making mistakes and learning from them.

Violet is the color of forgiveness. Its frequency is incompatible with blame or judgment. While you pray, you may wish to imagine yourself immersed in violet light or envision a violet flame consuming your body. This can turbocharge your prayer. I have included a sample prayer for forgiveness at the end of this chapter.

Prayers for Virtues

The Lord's Prayer is one of the greatest prayers ever spoken. It is also a prayer that focuses largely on the development of virtues. Unfortunately, the archaic language it uses limits our present-day understanding of its power. The Lord's Prayer was likely first uttered in Aramaic, a rich language with many nuances and inflections. It was first written down, however, in Greek, a much more highly structured language that robbed it of much of its meaning. This version was then translated into Latin, and finally into many other languages, including English.

Here, I have expressed the Lord's Prayer using words that can help revitalize its meaning and align that meaning with the shamanic path. If you are attached to a more traditional form of the prayer that has deep meaning for you, by all means continue to say it. Moreover, this simple rendition is just one out of many possibilities. Why not try your own hand at it?

SHAMANIC LORD'S PRAYER

The King James translation appears first in italics, followed by my shamanic version.

Our Father

Great Spirit, Creator, Source, Great Provider, Allah, Lord, Great Mother

Who art in heaven

Who is within us and everywhere right now

Hallowed be thy name

How infinitely great you are

Thy Kingdom come

Let your dream of awareness be realized

Thy will be done

Let your intention be realized

On Earth as it is in heaven

Here and now, everywhere in everything through our conscious awareness

Give us this day our daily bread

Thank you for all your blessings, all the resources you provide us

And forgive us our trespasses

Help us to forgive ourselves for mistakes and forgetfulness

As we forgive those who trespass against us

Help us to forgive those who forget their connection to Spirit

And lead us not into temptation

Guide us always on the path of compassion and right relationship

But deliver us from evil

Cleanse and protect us from injustice, hate, and suffering

For thine is the kingdom, and the power, and the glory

For you are the great truth, the conscious
awareness itself

For ever and ever, Amen

For ever and ever, Amen

PRAYER FOR WISDOM

Great Spirit,

I know and understand how to do many things.

Thank you for giving me the opportunities to learn.

But I know that knowledge doesn't make me wise.

You are the Source of all wisdom.

Please help me to follow in your footsteps.

Help me

To listen more,

To watch more,

To withhold my judgment,

To speak truth with courage,

To learn from wise people,

To cultivate silence.

And if I open myself to your wisdom,

I will become wise,

For you are with me always.

You teach me daily about truth, heart, and meaning.

I know that wisdom does not come all at once.

So *I Am* listening.

Great Spirit, I open my heart to you.

Thank you for helping me to withhold judgment,

To see with clarity,

To understand without confusion,

To be filled with awareness,

So that I may be generous and serve

And fulfill my life task work.

PRAYER FOR LOVE

Spirit, there have been times when I have forgotten that *I Am* loved.

And I have believed myself to be unloved,

Unworthy of love.

And I have fallen short of loving others.

And I have felt alone.

I have wondered if there was something wrong with me.

But I know there is nothing that I need to change to experience love.

Every minute, in this very minute, *I Am* surrounded by love.

You are love, and you live within my heart.

You fill every space with your creativity,

Fueled by love.

And all I need to do to return to that love

Is to remember it.

Spirit, I remember it now.

I Am loving.

I Am loved.

PRAYER FOR SELF-FORGIVENESS

Great Spirit,

There have been times when I have forgotten

That you are always with me, guiding me

Toward compassion, kindness, and care.

And I have made mistakes.

I worried and felt anxious.

I became angry and lost my temper.

I compared myself with others and came up short.

I thought I was lost and became afraid.

I thought I would fail.

I felt worthless.

I became discouraged and depressed.

I became envious and jealous.

I was afraid I would look like a fool in front of others.

I was critical and judged others.

I took foolish chances with my health and safety.

I refused to listen.

I was impatient with myself and with others.

And I lost my way because I fell asleep

And dreamed I was all alone in the vast Universe,

When the truth is that you are always with me.

And you never blamed me or judged me.

You make it possible for me to be forgiven

And to find the strength to forgive myself.

Spirit, I forgive myself with you as my witness.

I Am forgiven.

I Am loved.

I Am light as air, with a newness, a returning spring

Awakening in my heart.

And out of this dawning, this new day,

I forgive all those who have hurt me.

I forgive all those who have abandoned me.

I forgive all hurts real or imagined.

I Am letting go.

I Am releasing.

I Am free.

I Am free.

I Am free.

Chapter 10

Prayers for Others

If the only prayer you said was
thank you, that would be enough.
—Meister Eckhart

The Qero people live high in the Andes of Peru, in a mountain range between 14,000 and 17,000 feet high. They settled there when the Spanish conquistadores invaded their lands and tried to enslave and convert them. They were able to preserve their shamanic Incan spiritual practices because the Spanish horses could not climb to such heights, and they survived as a free people while other tribes were oppressed.

Some years ago, I received permission to visit the Qero with a small group that consisted of my family and a few friends. The experience was incomparable. One of the most powerful memories I have of that trip is witnessing the ability of the Qero *pacos* (shamans) to use prayer and coca leaves to change the weather. As a dangerous thunderstorm approached us with what seemed like inevitable force, they calmly whipped out their coca leaves and proceeded to petition the storm to alter its course and go around us. The raging storm immediately complied. My mouth fell open as the storm stopped in its tracks, and made one 90-degree turn and then another. After it had passed us, it made one last turn and left us behind unharmed—all while throwing deadly lightning bolts, roaring with rolling thunder, and dumping down torrential rain. Through all this, we were left completely dry and safe.

From my experience with the Qero, I learned that prayer can be used to control circumstances outside ourselves and to benefit others.

Helping Others

Shamanically speaking, praying for others is more complex than praying for yourself. Unless you know how to pray for yourself effectively, your efforts to help others will probably fail. But once you have learned to get results from your personal prayers, you can apply those lessons to praying for others. Here are some reasons why:

- First, you don't always know what is best for others, even if your intentions are good. Perhaps their own Essence, which is directly connected to Spirit, knows that an illness will teach them something they can learn in no other way. Perhaps it is simply their time to die and, no matter how much you pray, you will not be able to save them.

- Second, unless those you pray for want to be healed or helped in some way, they will not benefit from your prayers. Sometimes people have an agenda hidden in their illness or a problem that they may not want to give up. Perhaps they want to punish someone else by being sick or to make people feel sorry for them. Perhaps they feel so unworthy of help that they cannot conceive of receiving your assistance and block any path that might lead them out of their difficulty. There are many reasons why a person might not want to be helped or might not allow help in.

- Third, if you do not pray correctly for someone, you may actually do more harm than good. If you believe that without your help they will surely go under because they are weak and ineffective, you just pour energy into your skepticism about them, and this increases their difficulty.

You have to be careful when you pray for others. On the other hand, there are often excellent reasons to do so. Praying for others is a way of loving them. And almost everyone is in need of more love.

Sometimes, others may be in such a bad way that they are unable to pray for themselves, and your prayers can be powerfully effective in helping them out of a bad spot. If they are under anesthesia, or unconscious, or terribly anxious, or seriously depressed, or in terrific pain, they may be in great need your prayers. If your prayers for them are genuine and come from a loving state, they are never wasted. Even if others are not conscious of your prayers, your love does reach them and this helps, no matter what—even if they eventual die. By praying for them, you may make their death easier than it might have been without your intercession.

Here are some guidelines to help you pray for others in a powerful and effective way.

- Always ask permission from Spirit before you start praying for someone. Become quiet and go to the *I Am* place—the port in your heart where Essence connects. Then ask if your prayers are for that person's greatest good at this time. If you have trouble receiving a clear answer, notice if you receive a red or green light in response to your question.

If the light is green, pray away. If it is red, do not overrule it. Let the person be.

- If you receive permission to pray, ask Spirit to support your prayers and to grant the person for whom you are praying whatever he or she needs most at this time. Sometimes you may be shown exactly what to pray for; sometimes you won't.

- Go back to the *I Am* place and reconnect with your own Essence.

With the uncertainty of terrorism, war, and spreading disease that plagues our world today, you may be concerned about loved ones who are traveling afar or living in areas that have become dangerous. Of course, you cannot physically protect everyone you love or care for, but you can always turn to the power of prayer to assist them from within. Many young men and women have been protected in war zones and when on dangerous duty because someone far away prayed for and sent protection to them. Many Native American soldiers returned unscathed from horrific battles during World War II and Vietnam because they had shamans and family members praying for them and doing ceremony for them from afar. I give examples of this kind of prayer at the end of this chapter.

Balance, Harmony, and Peace

Sometimes you may wish to pray for something much bigger—like world peace, an end to hostilities between nations, or to relieve the suffering of the thousands who are in need of food or health care. Today, there is almost no limit to the number of world situations you can pray to heal. If you think that you are too inconsequential to have an impact on these great and sometimes remote world problems, you are wrong. Sincere prayers with strong intent coming from just one individual can have an amazing impact on the whole Universe. Chances are that others are praying to solve these problems as well, and their prayers will join yours, giving them greater impact. From a shamanic viewpoint, like attracts like.

While nature usually knows what it is doing and does not need any help, there are times when a little prayer can shift a storm just enough to protect you and your loved ones. The great master shamans all knew how to address the weather and bend it to their will when necessary. They knew that nature is in the domain of Spirit, so commanding the weather is like talking directly to God. To change or control conditions, therefore, you must address the weather itself. And you are much more likely to get results if you express gratitude and show respect.

Sometimes the environment suffers from too much rain, causing flooding, loss of life, and property damage. Likewise, while fire is good for the land, it can also be terribly destructive. The same is true for wind, cold, and heat. Fortunately, praying for relief and balance is no different than praying for abundance. Just approach Spirit with respect and gratitude, then state what is needed. While it may sound strange to you to address the elements directly, this is how it has always been done by shamans around the world. They know that the elements respond to human commands if given properly. That is why the Bible tells us that man was given dominion over the Earth—not to destroy or plunder it, but to work with it cooperatively.

Below, I give examples of prayers that you can use to restore balance to nature and control your environment.

PRAYER FOR HEALING OTHERS

The prayer below is specifically for migraines, but you can replace the word *migraines* with any other condition you may want to heal. This prayer may be successful the first time you use it. If not, don't be discouraged. Just persist with your shamanic praying.

Spirit, *I Am* praying for [Name].

I Am asking that he/she be healed of these painful migraines.

(Visualize darkness leaving from the person's head and dissipating in a violet flame. You can move your hands in a gesture to disperse the darkness and cast it into a candle flame if you like.)

Migraines, be gone from [Name]!

Migraines, leave [Name] now!

Migraines, you have no power over [Name]!

Spirit, allow [Name] at this time to learn whatever

The migraines have been trying to teach.

Allow [Name] to receive this information at the deepest levels of awareness

So this condition no longer prevails.

Send the most powerful inner specialists to work with [Name]

In order to bring healing.

May [Name] never experience this condition again.

The migraines are now gone, [Name]'s head feels bright and clear.

(Visualize the person smiling brightly and headache-free. Flood his or her head with bright metallic gold that is radiating a turquoise or green light.)

PRAYER TO PROTECT OTHERS

If you are praying to protect a loved one who may be in harm's way, try using the following prayer or something similar. Notice that the prayer actually directs Spirit toward what you want to accomplish.

Spirit, *I Am* praying for [Name].

I Am asking that [Name] be surrounded by your powerful protection.

Surround [Name] with your light.

(Visualize a bright electric-blue light of protection surrounding the person from head to foot.)

May [Name] always be protected and walk through danger unscathed.

May [Name] be safe to complete all goals and dreams.

May harmful actions and thoughts pass [Name] by.

Let [Name] walk in light and safety.

(Visualize the person walking safely through all challenges. Everything bounces off the surrounding protective blue light. Repeat this three times.)

PRAYER FOR PEACE

Gandhi once sagely said that, if you want something to become reality, you must first become it. If you want peace in the world, you must become it. That is why this prayer is structured the way it is. While it may sound odd, in fact it is designed to produce the maximum beneficial effect. And it becomes even more powerful when said in a group, with everyone participating in the vision of light spreading to wherever it is needed most.

Spirit, *I Am* praying for peace.

I Am light.

I Am light.

I Am light.

(Visualize a golden light burning in your chest, bright like the sun. Allow the sun to expand and fill your entire chest, then let it set the rest of your body on fire so that your entire being is radiating this golden light.)

Spirit, may there be peace in this world.

I Am peace.

(Repeat three times, then allow the golden light to expand out into the space all around you, and then outside your immediate vicinity to all the countryside and all the communities nearby.)

I Am light.

(Repeat three times.)

I Am peace.

(Repeat three times, then continue to see the golden light spreading from your chest out into the world, crossing mountains and oceans and spreading like a

wave around the globe. Allow this golden light to take on all the colors of the rainbow, bathing the areas that have special needs so that they can absorb exactly the colors they require.)

I Am light.

(Repeat three times.)

I Am peace.

(Repeat three times.)

I Am love.

(Repeat three times.)

You can continue this prayer for as long as you like. When you are ready, gradually return your mind to where you are sitting.

PRAYER FOR RAIN

Spirit, we see clouds gathering,

Heavy with life-giving rain.

And we know you are in these clouds,

Carrying the great gift of sweet water.

Thank you for this kindness.

Thank you for making the land green and rich.

Thank you for filling the rivers and lakes.

Thank you for providing us with water to drink.

Spirit in the clouds,

Send us the rain that we have been so in need of,

So all life may drink deeply.

Fill our streams and reservoirs.

We welcome this loving, nourishing gift.

We will not forget your generosity.

We are so fortunate.

We are so blessed.

We pray for rain.

We pray for rain.

We pray for rain.

Strongly visualize the clouds gathering and rain coming to the land. See drops of water bonding with tiny points of brilliant light. Feel gladness in your heart as you see, sense, and feel the fresh rain gathering into clouds and falling upon the landscape. Smell the new rain as it moisturizes the air and the soil, making everything fresh and nourished.

PRAYER FOR CONTAINING FIRE

Great Spirit,

You have given us a wonderful tool by giving us fire.

Fire warms us and is good for the land.

You gave us the fire of the sun that gives life.

You gave us the fire of our emotions.

You gave us the fire within each atom of our bodies.

You gave us the fire of electricity to light our way.

Spirit, thank you for this great gift you have given us.

Help us always to use this power wisely,

And protect us from fires that threaten us and our loved ones.

Sacred fire, powerful fire,

Bank your fierce flames so that we may live.

Be at rest and come no further.

Fire, I have asked Spirit to contain you.

Hear my prayer now.

Chapter 11

Advanced Prayer Techniques

The Great Spirit gave you two ears and only one mouth,
so you can talk half as much as you listen.

—Iroquois saying

In today's world of hectic scheduling and busy lives, people don't always have time for lengthy prayers, even though it would be an excellent practice to make time. A short prayer, even a phrase, can make a huge difference in your mood, your attitude, your perspective, your day, and your life. I have found this to be the case with all the phrases I give you in this section.

There are a couple of ways you can integrate these phrases into a regular routine that fits your busy schedule. You can use them anytime for a quick reminder of who you are and what you are about. This can help get you back on track if you have veered off it for a few hours and keep you focused on the golden line of your life. In fact, there is no limit to the number of times or how often you can repeat these phrases, as long as you are sure to focus your attention on what you are saying. When you just mouth them, they have very limited results. But when you give them your full attention, they will produce remarkable results. I guarantee it.

You can also use these phrases to prepare yourself for longer practices like meditation, contemplation, visualization, or longer prayers. They put you in the right frame of mind, return you to maximum effectiveness, and get you refocused on Essence and away from ego-oriented thoughts and feelings.

Words of Power

Here are some favorite phrases I have borrowed from great avatars, teachers, and mediums.

> *I Am* **the resurrection and the life.** This phrase, which was a favorite of Jesus, is a reminder that the responsibility to wake yourself up rests entirely with you. No one else, including any guru, saint, or avatar, will wake you up or resurrect you unless you ask for it. They can help if you want it enough, but it starts with you. Since the world you inhabit is generated entirely by your own experience, you are responsible for waking it

up. If you look around and say "this world sucks," then it does and this only reinforces the viewpoint of others who are convinced likewise. If you look around and say "all is sacred," then it is—not just for you, but for others who are willing to open their eyes and see that this is true. In other words, *every single person* is responsible for the resurrection and the life. Might as well get to it.

I Am **the light of the world.** This phrase, another favorite of Jesus, is a reminder that it is personal awareness that brings illumination to the physical world. Each person's awareness is the light of consciousness, and that consciousness is what activates the divine in everything. When you say "*I Am* the light of the world," you are telling the deepest truth. When you say these words, reality alchemically transforms the world to make it so.

I Am **the open door that no one can shut.** The "open door" is the portal in your mind that allows you to enter the higher vibrational realms. Specifically, it is located in the third ventricle of the brain, between the tips of your ears and behind the Third Eye located between your eyebrows (see chapter 4). It is a safe, neutral, and powerful place in which to house your awareness. By announcing "*I Am* the open door," you reinforce your belief that, like a shaman, you have a foot in both worlds—the physical world and the spiritual world from which all things come. By saying "that no one can shut," you indicate that, on the level of Essence, you are entirely in charge of this portal and nothing (especially the ego) can block you, control you, or prevent you from entering this higher dimension.

I Am **that I am.** This phrase is hard to understand unless we make one small, but important, addition: "*I Am so* that I am." Another way of expressing this is: God is, so that I am. The Infinite *I Am* (All that Is) makes it possible for the individual "I am" (me) to be here. The simple statement "God is, I am" has been referred to as the greatest sermon ever given.

The following are phrases that I learned from Paul Selig, a teacher and friend, master medium of the Guides, and author of many books, including *I Am the Word*, which I highly recommend.

I Am **in my knowing.** This affirms that you are connected with the supreme intelligence of the Universe. This intelligence is not dependent on content, ideas, concepts, or anything that has form. It is more like an empty container, a hollow bone or reed, whose value is its emptiness. This emptiness is part and parcel of the supreme intelligence.

I Am **in my loving.** This affirms that your heart is connected to the vibration of love, the great unifier, the Source of all life in the multiverse.

I Am **in my power.** This affirms that, on the level of Essence, you stand in your own power. That the ego does not control you. That you are free.

I have come to the Mansion. This affirms that you have entered the portal in the third ventricle of the brain referred to above (see also chapter 4).

I Am **free.** This affirms that, on the level of Essence, you are always free to choose. The ego thinks it is free, but it is not at all free to choose. It behaves more like a parasite that depends on its host to live. The ego can be overridden at any time by Essence.

I Am **here.** This simple affirmation reminds you that you have a body and you are in it, at this moment in time and space. In other words, it helps you to be present. To be here now. On a deeper level, it reminds you that you are *not* your ego. You are Essence, manifested right here and right now in physical form.

I know who *I Am.* This affirms that you are Spirit—God, All that Is, Source.

I know what *I Am.* This affirms that you are currently in a human body, albeit only temporarily.

I know how I serve. This affirms that you know what your medicine is. You know that blessing others with your medicine is your service.

I Am **known,** *I Am* **seen, and** *I Am* **heard by Spirit.** This affirms your unbreakable connection to Spirit in all you say and do.

The following phrases have a slightly different function from those above, in that they are meant to be used in specific situations. They are not so much prayers or affirmations as they are words to correct a situation that has become an obstacle to effective prayer.

Correct neutral now. This phrase means "Return my system to neutral right now." Use it when you are triggered or have lost your neutrality. If you are angry, anxious, depressed, or upset, hold up one hand vertically in front of your chest with the palm facing either left or right, depending on which hand you use, then say these words.

Oh, is that so? Use this phrase when you have been triggered, found yourself on one side of a polarized situation, or found yourself being very judgmental about something. It can help you return to a more neutral, non-judgmental mindset. For example, you may need to rebalance your mind after being triggered by a news broadcast, by something you read, or by something someone said to you. This phrase has amazing powers to bring you back to a neutral, and even slightly amused, state of mind.

Entering the Mansion

At the beginning of this book, I spoke about preparing for prayer and activating the Mansion (see chapter 4). This next practice takes you a step further and helps you to use the Mansion to transform your reality. It takes a lot of regular practice to master this technique, but it can usually be done without effort or struggle. It just takes attentiveness and focus for a few seconds each day—or maybe even several times a day.

As I explained earlier, in the very center of your head, behind your Third Eye, there is an empty space. This small open area is filled with a river of fluid that carries away toxins and brings in nutrients. All around it are the most important structures of the brain: the corpus callosum, the hippocampus, the amygdala, the ocular nerve, the cerebellum, the frontal lobe, the temporal lobes, the parietal lobes, the occipital lobe, the limbic lobe, and the white and gray matter. This is the Mansion of the Huichols, Paradise to the Toltecs.

Once you have located the Mansion, focus on it and use this short prayer to put yourself in the proper state of mind:

All is sacred, as am I.

All is holy, as am I.

All is divine, as am I.

As you recite this prayer, imagine a spinning golden egg that generates a beautiful golden light. This golden light extends and radiates out, surrounding your head and upper chest and creating a sense of calm serenity and neutrality.

This light activates a portal to other dimensions and an entrance to the world of Spirit. The place from which it emanates is personal and incompatible with fear, negativity, and egoic activity. In fact, fear ends when you enter the Mansion. Here there is no story and no ego, just stabilized, neutral, and blissful being. When you activate this, you may feel a buzzing in the top back of your head.

The light created by the spinning egg generates an extremely high vibrational field. Anything you lift up into it will be raised to a much higher vibration—transforming it alchemically from lead to gold, so to speak. In other words, any worries, concerns, obsessions, physical aches and pains, medical conditions, doubts, guilt, shame, anger, suffering, or fears you lift into this space are immediately accelerated to higher octaves. According to Paul Selig's Guides, any negative thoughts or behaviors you want to banish or transform or repurpose can be brought here to reconnect them with Spirit, which renders them powerless. The affirmation that expresses this repurposing is:

I make all things new.

When you enter the Mansion, you must do it in a spirit of loving-kindness, compassion, forgiveness, and generosity toward all beings and all elements of the environment. The Mansion has the power to banish or calm our personal demons, as well as those we project onto others. It is a wonderful place to go before praying, as well as an ideal place to remain throughout your prayers.

Working with *I Am*

We discussed the importance of the phrase *I Am* at the beginning of this book. Here I will show you how to use this phrase as a power tool. Remember, there is no other phrase quite as powerful for creating as *I Am*, because it aligns you with the Creator. When you say this phrase, you invoke your Essence, which goes way beyond your ego or false self. In spiritual literature, Essence is often referred to as Lord or Father. Shamans call it Spirit, the Black Eagle, the Central Sun, Great Provider, and many other names. You can call it whatever you wish, as long as you realize that it is the part of you that is connected directly to the Creator.

Here is a practice that can help you work with *I Am*. Do not approach this lightly, because the work is sacred and powerful and needs to be approached respectfully.

- Find a quiet place where you will not be interrupted. Lie down or sit if you can. Close your eyes except for a little slit.

- Begin by breathing deeply into your lungs.

- Place your attention on your chest—specifically, in the center of your heart. Imagine a single atom there that is the spark that generates your whole being. That atom is being given to you by the Creator at this very moment so you can become conscious and alive. Shamanically speaking, it is a tiny replica of the sun, to which it is connected energetically. Sense this connection with the powerful, radiant sun in the sky. They are one.

- As you breathe into the core of this atom then out again, say: *I Am.* You can say both words as you exhale, or you can say *I* as you inhale and *Am* as you exhale. Go slowly and savor each repetition. Try placing different emphasis on each word and sense what happens.

- When you feel ready, say: "*I Am* light." Envision a brilliant light being generated from the single atom—a light so bright that it expands out in blinding brilliance from your chest and sends rays out to every part of your body. You may experience this light expanding out in every direction, just like the sun—all through the community, the country, the world, and possibly out into the Universe. As it expands, it envelops all world leaders and enters their hearts, reminding them of the great loving light of Source.

- Now expand your statement to say: "*I Am* the light of the sun." Become a living, radiant, glowing sun and continue sending your light to the places in greatest need. Try linking this sun to all the other suns in the cosmos and be aware that all these suns are radiating their light back to you. This will enhance the power of this process.

- Feel the power of being created each second. Sense that being awake and aware is a fabulous blessing. Thank Spirit for creating you.

- When you are ready, say: "*I Am* the light of the world." Be aware of the profound miracle of being alive, conscious, and aware, but without thoughts.

- Focus on the point in the middle of your heart and be aware of how good it feels to be there. Try pressing on your sternum where you feel good. Stay with this as long as you like. Do it often, and miracles will definitely happen.

Waking Up

Waking up shamanically and spiritually involves a great many variables, including your actual readiness, your maturity, your experience, your desire, your feelings of worthiness, and a host of other influences. If you have read this far in this book, you have probably already awakened to some degree. But there are techniques that can help you become more fully awake.

One profound practice is to locate and become aware of the *medulla oblongata*, the area where your spine enters your skull at the base of the brain. You can find pictures of this in most anatomy books or on the Internet. The medulla oblongata is like a little snake with a flower on the end. In spiritual literature, this flower has been referred to as the "mouth of God." Paramahansa Yogananda and many other great spiritual teachers have spoken about the significance and importance of this structure to consciousness. The following practice is a powerful technique that was recommended in part by Paramahansa Yogananda himself.

- Sit quietly in an undisturbed place; breathe regularly into your chest and focus on your heart.

- As you breathe out say: "*I Am*" several times.

- Now focus on the base of your brain and envision a brilliant golden light there.

- As you breathe out, say: "*I Am*." You may find it helpful to imagine the words printed on the base of your brain at the location of the medulla.

- Now focus on the point between your eyebrows and imagine rays of brilliant golden light streaming from the little flower at the top of the medulla, upward toward your mostly closed eyes. Allow the rays to stream out of your eyes.

- Now imagine a third ray streaming out of your Third Eye, forming a little triad of rays from your medulla, from your eyes, and from your Third Eye.

- Allow a portion of this light to bounce back to the medulla to set up a circular flow of golden light.

- Continue for as long as you wish.

Remember that you are working with very powerful forces here. If you are not ready, you will experience nothing. If you are ready, however, you will experience an expansion of your awareness and consciousness.

A Powerful Walking Meditation

When you are out for a walk or a hike, you can practice this very simple exercise to wake up. Begin with softly reciting or just thinking the word "Here" on every other step. For example, if you start walking on your right foot then every time you take a step with your right foot, say "Here." Pay attention and notice that you are here even though you are moving. Do this for as long as you wish.

Next, take one step with your right foot and say, "Here," but then on the next step taken with your right foot say, "Now." Alternate the two. Pay attention to being here and now. Do this for a while.

Next add the word "New" to the sequence, again only when taking a step with the right foot . So now you are saying "Here," "Now," "New" in a kind of cadence as you walk. Notice that you are always a fresh and new being as you walk. Do this for a while.

Finally add the word "Free" to the cadence, so that you are saying "Here," "Now," "New," "Free" on each subsequent step you take with your right foot. See if you can attend to the meaning of each word as you go. Should you notice that you've started to just repeat the words in an absentminded, unconscious way, take a break from the exercise.

You can play with alternating the words in a different order to see what happens. The main thing to realize is that all the words are referencing something that is absolutely true.

Conclusion

Nothing you have read in this book is new. All the information is as old as the proverbial hills. I have just presented it in a way that is perhaps new and more accessible for you. These prayers found their way into my life, and now I have passed them on to you so you can build your own spontaneous prayers and vastly transform your experience of Spirit within your life.

Without prayer, our lives can be a great struggle that rages without direction or support. With prayer, this dynamic changes radically to one of evolving participation and quantum leaps of awakening. Praying is, quite literally, talking to Spirit in a way that launches us into the main current of our life-stream. It quickens our minds, opens our hearts, and prompts a powerful development that makes life a dance in the garden rather than a crawl through the briars.

The great shamans and saints have all said that their prayers led them ever deeper into a life of communing with Spirit and listening for the great wisdom that emerged from their after-prayer silence. May you also be showered with such blessings and exalted by such graces.

Acknowledgments

I wish to acknowledge all those students who participate in my shamanic study programs, all those who
attend my workshops and webinars, all those who
join me in remote healings, pilgrimages, and travel
adventures, and all those who work so hard to grow
through my counsel. May you all receive 10,000
blessings and the prayers that you so richly deserve.

About the Author

José Luis Stevens has completed a ten-year apprenticeship with a high-degree Huichol shaman living in the Sierras of Mexico and has specific training with Shipibo shamans in the Amazon and in the Andes regions of Peru. He has studied with and visited shamans in Central Australia, Nepal, Finland, and the American Southwest. He holds a doctorate in counseling psychology from the California Institute of Integral Studies, as well as a master's in clinical social work from the University of California, Berkeley. He runs a coaching and consulting business based on the principles outlined in his books and brings over fifty years of experience to his many clients through effective guidance programs, retreats, trainings, and seminars.

He and his wife Lena are the founders of The Power Path School of Shamanism, which provides webinars, articles, forecasts, and a wide variety of shamanic information. They are the authors of *Secrets of Shamanism: Tapping the Spirit Power Within You* (Avon, 1988). In addition to numerous other books and articles, Stevens is the author of *Encounters with Power* (Sounds True, 2016), *Awaken the Inner Shaman* (Sounds True, 2014), *The Power Path: The Shaman's Way to Success in Business and Life* (New World Library, 2002), and *Transforming Your Dragons: How to Turn Fear Patterns into Personal Power*, released in 1994 by Bear and Company.

Stevens's base of operations is in Santa Fe, New Mexico. He lectures internationally on a number of topics, including principles of power, prosperity, personality types, communication styles, peak performance, and self-development. He has consulted with individuals and businesses in Japan, Canada, Venezuela, Iceland, England, and Finland, and both he and Lena have led many tour groups to the ancient sacred sites of Egypt, England, Mexico, Guatemala, and Peru.

Stevens consults with lawyers, business leaders, scientists, life coaches, spiritual teachers, and entrepreneurs from coast to coast, as well as with producers, actors, and screenwriters. He uses his knowledge of shamanism and business psychology to coach and assist leaders in making difficult life decisions and developing business strategies. Learn more about his work at *www.thepowerpath.com*.

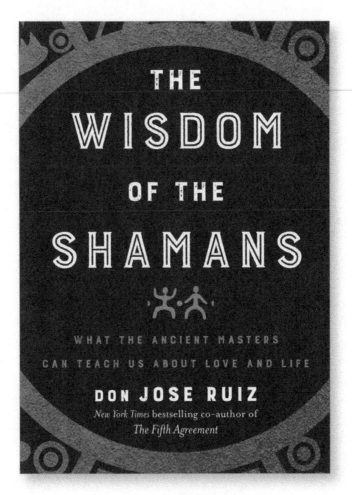

Hierophant publishing

books that inspire your body, mind, and spirit

Hierophant Publishing
8301 Broadway, Suite 219
San Antonio, TX 78209
888-800-4240

www.hierophantpublishing.com